CONTENTS

INTRODUCTION 10

Identification 12–14
Butterfly or Moth 14
Lifecycle 16–19
Behavior 20
Habitat 22
Survival 23
Conservation 25
Using this Guide 25

PAPILIONIDAE—SWALLOWTAILS 30–43

Pipevine Swallowtail 32
Polydamas Swallowtail 33
Blue Triangle 34
Scarce Swallowtail 36
Giant Swallowtail 37

Tiger Swallowtail 38
Swallowtail 39
Black Swallowtail 40
Apollo 42
Southern Festoon 43

PIERIDAE—WHITES AND SULFURS 44–67

Black-veined White 46
Wood White 47
Large White/Cabbage White 48
Green Veined White 50
Small White 51
Bath White 52
Orange Sulfur 54

Clouded/Common Sulfur 55
Clouded Yellow 56
Pale Clouded Yellow 58
Cleopatra 59
Brimstone 60
Orange Tip 62
Tiger Pierid 64
Orange-barred Giant Sulfur 66

LYCENIDAE—GOSSAMER WINGS 68–93

Green Hairstreak 70
Atala 71
Purple Hairstreak 72
Gray Hairstreak 74
White Letter Hairstreak 75
Brown Hairstreak 76
Large Copper 77
Small Copper 78
Sooty Copper 80
Brown Argus 81

Holly Blue 82
Eastern Tailed Blue 83
Longtailed Blue 84
Large Blue 85
Adonis Blue 86
Acmon Blue 88
Silver Studded Blue 89
Idas Blue 90
Common Blue 92
Duke of Burgundy Fritillary 93

NYMPHALIDAE—BRUSHFOOTS 94–156

White Peacock 96
Purple Emperor 98
Hackberry Butterfly 99
The Viceroy 100
Red Lacewing 102
Owl Butterfly 104
Two-tailed Pasha 105
Painted Lady 106
Baltimore Checkered 108
Peacock 110
Buckeye 111
Indian Leaf Butterfly 112
White Admiral 114
Southern Snout Butterfly 115
Blue Morpho 116
Malachite 118
Common Glider 119
Cardinal 120
Clipper 121
Pearl Crescent 122
Comma 124
Mother-of-Pearl Butterfly 125
Red Admiral 126

Indian Red Admiral 128
Queen of Spain Fritillary 130
Silver washed Fritillary 131
Silver-bordered Fritillary 132
Lesser Marbled Fritillary 134
Marsh Fritillary 136
Spotted Fritillary 137
Great Spangled Fritillary 138
Regal Fritillary 140
Small Tortoiseshell 141
Mourning Cloak/
Camberwell Beauty 142
Large Tortoiseshell 144
Gulf Fritillary 145
Julia/Flambeau 146
Zebra 147
Heliconius Mimic 148
The Postman 150
Sweet Oil 152
Plain Tiger 153
Queen 154
Monarch 156

HESPERIIDAE—SKIPPERS 158–169

Arctic Skipper 160
Silver Spotted Skipper 161
Large Skipper 162
Dingy Skipper 164

Grizzled Skipper 165
Lulworth Skipper 166
European Skipper 168
Long-tailed Skipper 169

SATYRIIDAE—SATYRS AND BROWNS 170–187

(European) Ringlet 172
Pearly Heath 173
Small Heath 174
(American) Ringlet 175
Little Wood Satyr 176
Grayling 178

Gatekeeper 179
Meadow Brown 180
Marbled White 182
Dryad Butterfly 184
Speckled Wood 185
Wall Brown 186

MOTHS 188–237

Garden Tiger Moth 190

Giant Leopard Moth 191

White Ermine 192

Silkmoth 194

Owl Moth 196

Large Emerald 198

Brindled Beauty 199

Swallowtailed Moth 200

Eastern Tent Caterpillar
Moth 202

Lappet Moth 203

Oak Eggar 204

Gypsy Moth 206

Black Witch 208

Giant Agrippa 209

Puss Moth 210

White plume Moth 211

Indian Meal Moth 212

Regal Moth 214

Promethea Moth 216

Io Moth 217

Atlas Moth 218

American Moon Moth 220

Indian Moon Moth 222

Great Peacock Moth 223

Polyphemus Moth 224

Emperor Moth 226

Cecropia/Robin Moth 227

Hornet Moth 228

Death's Head Hawk Moth
230

Hummingbird Clearwing 231

Carolina Sphinx 232

Webbing/Common Clothes
Moth 234

Madagascan Sunset Moth 236

Family Groups 238–247

Glossary 248–252

Index 253

Picture Credits 256

INTRODUCTION

B utterflies and moths tend to elicit a range of emotions in us, from wonder at their incredible beauty, their ability to metamorphose or their unbelievable feats of physical achievement, to dismay at their voracious appetites for our crops and clothing. For many of us, simply observing butterflies skipping across the flowers in our yards is pleasure enough; however, the world of butterflies and moths is full of remarkable and often unknown facts and details.

Butterflies and moths belong to the order Lepidoptera. This Greek word translates as "scales" and "wing": the most obvious feature that separates them from other orders of insects is their scaled wings. There are in excess of 160,000 known species of Lepidoptera in the world, and only about 10 percent of these are butterflies. They can survive in an incredibly diverse range of habitats, from frozen Arctic tundra to high-altitude mountain slopes to humid rainforests. It is perhaps this diversity and adaptability that has enabled the Lepidoptera to survive on the planet for the last 140 million years. The first Lepidoptera were primitive moths; butterflies evolved around 40 million years ago.

The object of this book is to provide a glimpse into the fascinating world of butterflies and moths, using a very small selection of the known species that currently inhabit our planet. Each butterfly entry points out the significant features of an individual species which can either aid identification or simply illustrate some of its more interesting attributes.

Right: A Malachite butterfly (Metamorpha stelenes) on a leaf with its wings closed. Its common name comes from the beautiful green of its wings with their strong veining, which is reminiscent of the semi-precious stone malachite.

Above: Lepidoptra have two pairs of wings with a wide range of different colors and patterns that are an important factor when identifying the species.

Identification

Butterflies and moths are members of the insect class, sharing the same key features of three pairs of legs and three body parts: head, thorax, and abdomen. In addition to these features, Lepidoptera also have two pairs of wings, the forewings and hindwings, which are covered with scales. These scales reflect light, revealing the colors and patterns that are so important when identifying different species. The pair of antennae on the head of the butterfly is the primary sense organ, receiving smells, pheromones, and vibrations. A butterfly's proboscis is its tongue, enabling it to suck up food, nutrients, and moisture. It is hollow and contains two parallel tubes; the end bears the taste sensors. Different species will have different lengths of proboscis: some members of the hawk moth family have a proboscis that exceeds their own body length and is capable of piercing fruit or beehives, whereas others, such as the luna moths, have no mouthparts at all and cannot feed as adults. Another organ is the labial palps, used to clean the proboscis and eyes and to sense and taste food; the American Snout butterfly has particularly large palps. The head also bears a pair of compound eyes, capable of detecting color and movement. The jointed legs contain sensors at the "feet" which enable a butterfly to identify the plant it has just landed on, particularly important for females that need to lay eggs on a specific host plant.

Probably the first point of observation when identifying a butterfly or moth is the color and patterning that is displayed on the wings. When a butterfly is in flight this can be particularly difficult to do; it is when at rest that we get the opportunity to closely examine the markings of a particular species. Look for the coloring, any significant patterns, eyespots or markings. The majority of butterflies hold their wings closed above their bodies, leaving only the underside visible; some will hold their wings out flat, perhaps sunning themselves, affording us a glimpse of their often more brightly colored upper side. The color of the body can also be a useful feature: many species show abdomens that are highly colored or banded, or have markings on the head or thorax. The keen lepidopterist should also notice the size and shape of the butterfly, whether there are any wing streamers, or tails, and the general shape of the wings: broad, narrow, pointed, rounded, scalloped, or fringed.

Below: The size and shape of a butterfly's body and wings are also a clue to identification. This Nymph Sailor (Neptis hylas) has pointed forewings and rounded hindwings.

Be aware when attempting identification that individual species can vary in appearance. Newly emerged or fresh butterflies can have brighter colors, whereas older specimens can have faded wings, or even show wear and tear. Butterflies appearing in different seasons can vary, and many species can vary depending on whether they are from a first brood or a later one. Males and females of the same species can also differ, either completely or only slightly, perhaps in size or tone. Then of course there are butterflies that vary between different regions, confusingly appearing in a number of different forms. Where appropriate, any differences in appearance have been included in the descriptions provided here.

Butterfly or moth?

In some respects the differences between butterflies and moths may seem rather arbitrary. Although moths are regarded as the butterflies' less coloful, less attractive cousins, there are a great many beautiful, highly colored daytime-flying moths. Conversely, a large number of butterflies can appear rather dull and insignificant, and are often mistaken for moths. There are, however, a number of general features that separate moths from butterflies.

Butterflies are diurnal—daytime—fliers, whereas the great majority of moths are nocturnal, flying and (if appropriate) feeding at night. They also differ structurally: when resting, the wings of butterflies are usually held together upward over the back of the body, whereas moths will fold their wings flat across the body, the hindwing tucked beneath the forewing. In flight, the wings of the moth are "coupled" together with the use of special bristles on the hindwing which catch hold of the forewing. Butterflies lack this feature; instead their hindwing is expanded underneath the forewing, providing support with which to fly. The

Above: Butterflies, such as this Monarch (Danaus plexippus), typically rest with their wings upright and have slender antennae that are clubbed at the end. They also tend to have more slender bodies than moths, which are often stocky in shape.
Opposite: Eastern Tiger Swallowtails (Papilo glaucus) in two different colors.

antennae of each also differ: butterflies have very slender antennae which are clubbed at the end; moths lack this clubbing, having either slim or feathered antennae. Butterflies also tend to have more slender bodies, whereas some moths can be very stocky and broad in shape. There are, of course, exceptions to all these rules: the colorful daytime moths of the Uranidae family and the Australian Regent Skipper butterfly with its moth-like wing-coupling device are just two examples among many.

Conservation

With so many different species of butterfly and moth in existence, it can be hard to believe that they are seriously threatened. However, a number of fascinating and beautiful butterflies and moths are in peril, from either habitat change or over-zealous collectors. As people become increasingly interested in observing and recording sightings of butterflies, efforts to conserve species have increased.

Loss of native habitats is the most serious threat. On a large scale, massive deforestation, such as in Central America and Asia, can affect many different species. However, even on a small scale, many butterflies rely on plants that we consider weeds, such as nettles, thistles, or dandelions. The use of pesticides can have a harmful effect on some species, and pesticides that target destructive butterflies, such as the Gypsy moth, are also responsible for the near-eradication of other, innocent, species. There are some conservation measures in place: many species are legally protected from collectors; others have been reintroduced into native environments. However, many butterflies and moths remain under threat of extinction.

Using this guide

The entries provide a tiny example of the more common or unusual butterfly and moth species. Each entry contains a general description of the butterfly: where it is a uniform pattern or color just the upper side is described, but if there is a difference between upper and lower sides this is clearly explained. Differences between the sexes are also described, although only one example may be seen in the picture. Other information included can be useful for identification purposes: the average wingspan of the adult, its typical habitat and range, and the likelihood of observing it—its "status." Brief details on the caterpillar and its host plant are provided, since this can enhance identification; many butterflies choose to live in habitats where their larval host plant is found. The entries are organized into butterflies and moths, then into each major family. The huge numbers of moths mean only a small sample of the many families is represented here. Large families of butterflies are organized into sub-families. All the entries use the species' common name, which can vary from region to region; scientific names are consistent across the world.

*Opposite: A Queen Butterfly (*Danaus gilippus*) resting on a flower.*

THE LIFE OF
THE BUTTERFLY

LIFE-CYCLE

There are four stages in the life cycle of all Lepidoptera—egg, caterpillar, pupa, and butterfly—and each stage is vital. Butterflies are not simply attractive pollinators of garden flowers: their ultimate goal is to mate and successfully reproduce; likewise, caterpillars must not only feed and store up energy, they also have to ensure they are not the victims of hungry predators.

Laid singly, in small groups or in huge numbers, eggs can take either a few days or several weeks to hatch. They can be one of a number of shapes, colors and even sizes: some eggs are tiny, others surprisingly large. Eggs are usually laid on specific host plants by the female butterfly, which walks across the plant surface using the sensors in her legs to determine it is the correct one. Less fussy eggs can be released in flight, particularly those whose caterpillars feed upon grass. Once the egg hatches, the newly emerged caterpillar begins by eating the hard shell, then it gets to work eating its host plant.

Above: The eggs of a Large White (Pieris brassicae) on a leaf.
Opposite: The pupa is vulnerable to predators, so it is often very well camouflaged to look like the fruit or bud on a plant.

Caterpillars also appear in a wide variety of sizes, shapes, and colors. They are particularly vulnerable to predators: birds, other insects and lizards are among the many animals that prey on these butterfly larvae, and so their appearance is often determined by their need to protect themselves. Poisonous caterpillars may appear brightly colored to ward off attack, or bear aggressive spines that can irritate if touched or ingested. The caterpillars of the Arctid moth family are particularly hairy and collectively referred to as "woolly bears." Some caterpillars display very unusual and somewhat aggressive features, such as horns, alarming tail whips, and false eyespots. Many Swallowtail caterpillars have an organ called an osmaterium, rather like an inflatable horn, which releases a repulsive scent. The caterpillar of the Puss moth has a number of these aggressive attributes, and can also spit formic acid for good measure. Many other caterpillars adopt rather more passive but equally successful methods of protecting themselves from predators, either adopting camouflage or simply hiding within or beneath the foliage.

Caterpillars spend most of their time eating, and as their bodies grow they slough off their skin, rather like a snake. Most caterpillars will shed their skin several times before they are large enough to begin pupating. For most species, this means that the final skin-shedding reveals not another caterpillar but its chrysalis or cocoon. For others, particularly moths, the chrysalis is spun from a single strand of silk, encasing the caterpillar in a protective shell so that it can begin its transformation.

Once the caterpillar has revealed or spun its chrysalis, it enters the pupa stage. As a pupa, it is extremely vulnerable to predators since it is completely immobile; consequently pupae will adopt a number of strategies to protect themselves. Most pupae are incredibly well camouflaged, resembling dry leaves, twigs, fresh buds, and even bird droppings, such as those of the Swallowtail family. Some pupa casings are covered with spines while others containing a poisonous butterfly will advertise their inedible status. Many species pupate underground, within plant roots or even inside ants' nests, such as the Large Blue butterfly pupa. It usually takes around two weeks for

*Opposite: Caterpillar of a Monarch butterfly (*Danaus plexippus*) on milkweed.*
Right: The wing colors of a Monarch can clearly be seen through this transparent chrysalis.

pupation to complete, although some species can take much longer—several months or even two years, depending on external circumstances.

Once metamorphosis is complete, the butterfly must break out of the chrysalis. At this stage the wings are crumpled up; it is the body that must be forced out of the shell. As the butterfly takes in air for the first time, its thorax and abdomen can expand and its wings can begin to swell. The wings are composed of two membranes which are fed by veins, and as these fill up so the wings are expanded to take on their final shape. However, before it flies, the fresh butterfly must allow its wings to dry out and harden, a process that can take several hours.

Behavior

The lifespan of a butterfly varies from species to species. Some live for less than a week, others long enough to migrate through the winter months. But the typical adult butterfly will, during its lifetime, fly, feed, mate, and migrate.

Feeding butterflies use their proboscis to suck up liquid nutrients such as flower nectar, tree sap, rotten fruit juices, honeydew, blood, and faecal liquid and even, in some cases, animal tears. Some male butterflies, such as the Blue Triangle, will feed from the mud found in puddles or on riverbanks, probably seeking extra nutrients necessary for reproduction.

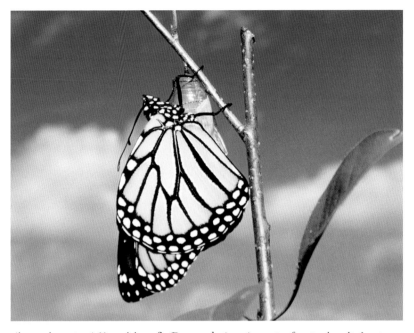

*Above and opposite: A Monarch butterfly (*Danaus plexippus*) emerging from its chrysalis. Its wings have been crumpled inside so the butterfly must rest to allow them to expand and harden.*

Reproduction can only take place when butterflies of the same species successfully identify one another. This can be particularly tricky when different species look similar or when the environment makes it awkward to spot a potential mate. Some butterflies are dependent upon their pheromones or scent to entice their partner, others will engage in elaborate courtship displays which communicate compatibility as well as general suitability. Mating pairs will clasp together, either landed or in air, and can remain attached for anything from twenty minutes to twenty-four hours. The male then usually heads off in search of a new mate while the female begins to search for a suitable place to deposit her eggs.

The majority of butterflies remain within the same territory for their whole lives, being able to satisfy their needs within their chosen habitat and range. However, some species migrate across relatively long distances in order to take advantage of potential food sources in other areas. During warm periods butterflies will migrate in order to follow the fine weather; for instance, the Monarch, a well-

known migrant, will head north across the North American continent, following the spread of new flowers brought by spring. In most cases, the butterflies that migrate out of their range do not return home; instead the next generation heads back to the native area as the seasons change. In Europe, well known migrant butterflies include Pale Clouded Yellows and Painted Ladies; these are generally native to North Africa and Mediterranean Europe but can regularly be found as far north as Scandinavia during the summer months. Other butterflies, such as the Red Admiral, migrate in order to overwinter, or to hibernate. They seek out temperate but cool climates where they can remain, safely immobile, reserving their energy until the arrival of spring. The onset of winter is a challenge that all species of butterfly and moth have to face. Different species cope with this period when little or no food is available in particular ways. Many overwinter as eggs, or choose this time to pupate; those that are already adults may hibernate; some caterpillars, too, are able to shut down their metabolism to wait out the winter months.

Habitat

The relationship between butterflies and their habitat is crucial; particular habitats are chosen by individual species because they have evolved adaptations suitable to those habitats.

All Lepidoptera need warmth to provide them with the energy to fly; therefore butterflies are found in sunny, tropical, and temperate regions. They will need specific foods both for breeding and for the adults to feed. Typical habitats will therefore be places such as open woodland, where the sunlight can penetrate and where there are plentiful flowers, or meadows and grassland, heathland and coasts with their specific flora, or mountain slopes. Powerful butterflies will survive in forest or woodland canopies, living up at the treetops; weak fliers prefer to stay closer to the ground amongst shrubs and trees which will provide protection from winds. Butterflies found in woodland will often be colored red, brown, or gray, so they resemble dry leaves or bark; others are bright green, like fresh leaves. Butterflies are dependent upon these particular places, and the loss of native habitats can only have dire consequences for their numbers.

Opposite: A fully emerged Monarch. The loss of their native habitat has a major impact on the survival of some butterfly species. Many will only feed on one particular plant or have adapted so successfully that they cannot survive in an alternative area.

Survival

With so many potential predators, butterflies and moths employ a number of techniques to aid survival. Many species are inedible; their caterpillars feed from host plants that contain poisons, storing these in their bodies so that the adult butterfly can benefit from the chemicals: the members of the Heliconius sub-family contain the poisons found in the larval food plant, passionflower (*passiflora*). Poisonous butterflies advertise this fact to birds, lizards, and other insects with their brightly colored and patterned wings. Many edible butterflies take advantage of these poisonous species by copying their appearance; this technique is known as mimicry. Butterflies will mimic others for one of two reasons: either to appear to be poisonous when not, as does the non-poisonous mimic of the Monarch, the Viceroy, or to emphasize their own poisonous status.

Edible species that do not mimic use other tactics. Many will adopt camouflage as an effective technique to avoid becoming prey; the Indian Leaf butterfly is an excellent example of this, as are a number of moths, including the Brindled Beauty. Others will use their wing markings to confuse or frighten

Above: Nymph butterfly on flowers.
Opposite: Some butterflies and moths, such as this Polyphemus moth (Antherea polyphemus), are well camouflaged so it can be difficult for them to find a mate by sight. For this reason, many species rely on their pheromones, or carry out elaborate courtship displays.

predators. Distinctive markings can suggest an even larger predator is at hand; the owl face seen by the enemy is simply the wings of the Owl Butterfly, the snake's head among the leaves is actually the hooked forewing of the Atlas moth. Eyespots are a particularly effective way of confusing and warding off enemies; some butterflies, such as the Blue Morpho, have a solid color on their upper-side but large eyespots from below which startle a predator when they are flashed unexpectedly. Butterflies that use eyespots to frighten their enemies, such as the Peacock, can often find themselves with ragged wings as a result of inquisitive pecks from confused birds. Although dangerous, these pecks warn the Peacock of danger, giving it time to fly away.

PAPILIONIDAE
SWALLOWTAILS

PIPEVINE SWALLOWTAIL BATTUS PHILENOR

CATERPILLAR: Ruddy brown body with a line of red or black tentactles along the back. Feeds mainly on pipevines, but will eat other plants
WINGSPAN: 2³⁄₄–4³⁄₈ inches
HABITAT: Meadows, riversides, urban yards and roadsides; mountainous forest in the east, desert in the west
RANGE: Central states of North America down toward Central America
STATUS: More common further south

Swallowtails are so called because of the "tails" that emerge from their hindwings. The Pipevine Swallowtail has broad, pointed forewings and rounded hindwings with gentle scallops and short tails. The forewings are a dull, blackish color and the hindwings are an iridescent blue with pale creamy markings on the upper side. The underside of the hindwings is blue, marked with a row of seven large, black-ringed orange spots. Females are duller and lack the blue sheen seen on the males. The caterpillar's almost exclusive diet of pipevine leaves makes both it and the adult butterfly poisonous, and as a result the butterfly is the model for mimics such as the Tiger Swallowtail.

BATTUS POLYDAMUS POLYDAMUS SWALLOWTAIL

Sometimes called the Tailless Polydamus, the Polydamus Swallowtail occurs in a number of regional forms but all members of this species share some key features. It has scalloped hindwings with no tails; its background color is dark, almost black, often with a green sheen on the hindwings. There is a bright yellow band on each wing and yellow edges to the hindwings. The underside of the hindwing is marked with red spots or crescents, and its black body can often be spotted with red. The caterpillar feeds on poisonous plants, making both the pupa and the butterfly inedible for birds.

CATERPILLAR: Yellow body covered with fine black striping on each segment. Feeds on pipevines

WINGSPAN: $2^{3}/_{4}$–$3^{1}/_{2}$ inches

HABITAT: Open woodland, urban yards and parks, forest canopies

RANGE: Southern states of North America down into Central and South America and the Caribbean

STATUS: Common and widespread, the Polydamus adapts well to different environments

BLUE TRIANGLE

GRAPHIUM SARPEDON

The Blue Triangle has long triangular forewings and relatively long, scalloped hindwings, but no tail. Its body and background color are black; it has distinctive and striking bands of translucent blue-green across both wings, and these are marked with delicate black veins. There are also blue-green crescents marking the outer edges of the hindwings. Males have scent sacs on the inner edge of the hindwings which enable differentiation from the otherwise similar females.

CATERPILLAR: Green body with yellow stripes along its sides and short spines on the front and the back. Feeds on a variety of trees, including camphor, laurel, and myrtle
WINGSPAN: 2³⁄₈–3¹⁄₂ inches
HABITAT: Open woodland, riverbanks, clearings, and lowland forests
RANGE: From India to China and Japan, Malaysia and Australasia
STATUS: Common. In some areas the caterpillar is considered a pest

SCARCE SWALLOWTAIL IPHICLIDES PODALIRIUS

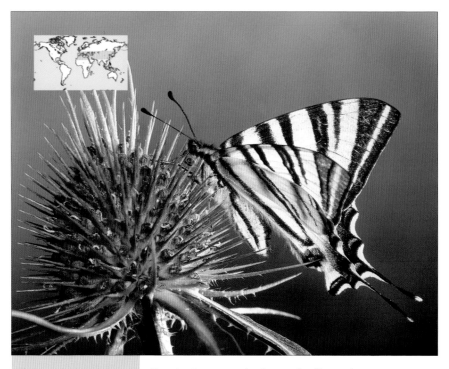

CATERPILLAR: Plump and green with yellow stripes, sometimes spotted red. Feeds on sloe and blackthorn

WINGSPAN: 2¾–3½ inches

HABITAT: Yards, fields and open woodland

RANGE: Across central and southern Europe to China and Asia and north Africa

STATUS: Generally widespread and common; however in some areas of central Europe its habitat is under threat

Despite its name, the Scarce Swallowtail is a common sight in Europe. It has a creamy yellow background color marked with striking dark bars. Some species have an almost white background color with black stripes. The wedge-shaped stripes are wider toward the forewing, and the margins of both wings are lined with black. The hindwings are scalloped and have long streamers which are black with yellow edging. The scalloped margins are marked with blue spots and there is a red-orange and blue eyespot on the inner edge of the hindwing. They can easily be observed feeding on flowers, often lavender, with a floating, smooth flight.

PAPILIO CRESPHONTES GIANT SWALLOWTAIL

This black and yellow swallowtail is one of the largest butterflies that inhabits North America and is found particularly in the southern states, where its caterpillars are considered to be a pest in areas where citrus fruit is grown. The butterfly can be distinguished by the diagonal band of yellow spots on each forewing. Large yellow spots also line the margins of each wing and there are yellow eyespots on the tails. Its background color is black, as is its upper body; however its abdomen is yellow with a central black streak. Two small red and black eyespots mark the inner edge of each hindwing.

CATERPILLAR: Brown with irregular white marks. It feeds on wild plants, citrus and plants in yards, and is considered a pest in orange groves

WINGSPAN: 4–6 inches

HABITAT: Woodland, orchards, yards, and lowlands.

RANGE: Central America up to southern states of North America, particularly Florida and Texas

STATUS: Common in localized areas

TIGER SWALLOWTAIL PAPILIO GLAUCUS

CATERPILLAR: Leaf green and plump, the caterpillar is excellently camouflaged. Feeds on trees, particularly cherry, willow and ash
WINGSPAN: 3½–6¾ inches
HABITAT Woodland, wooded gardens and parks
RANGE: Across the North American continent, from Alaska and Canada to Mexico
STATUS: Widespread and common

The yellow- and black-striped appearance of this swallowtail has resulted in its popular name of "tiger." Its background color is yellow with black stripes on the forewing and black wing margins lined with yellow spots. It has a black V-shaped marking on the hindwing, its tail streamers are black and its hindwing edges are gently scalloped. Its abdomen is black with yellow stripes, matching the wings. Males and females are generally similar; however in some more southern females the yellow markings are lacking, with some purely black examples. These darker butterflies are believed to be mimicking the highly poisonous Pipevine Swallowtail (*Battus philenor*).

PAPILIO MACHAON OLD WORLD SWALLOWTAIL

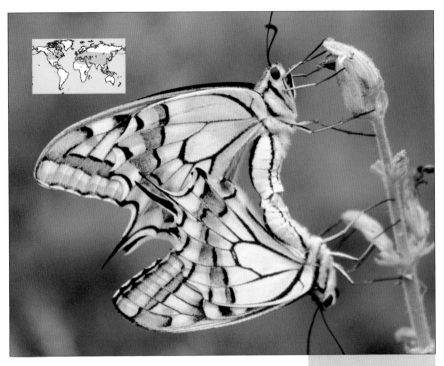

Referred to as the "Old World Swallowtail" in the United States and the Swallowtail in Europe, this butterfly is widespread across the temperate Northern Hemisphere. It has distinctive and easily recognized patterning and short, delicate tail streamers. The background color of the wings is a creamy yellow which is marked with black veins. The outer margins of the forewings are lined with black, lined in turn with yellow spots. The marginal band on the hindwing is blue-black, with a red eyespot in each corner. This swallowtail is a particularly strong, fast flier.

CATERPILLAR: Bright green with black stripes spotted with red. Feeds on carrot, milkweed, dill, and fennel

WINGSPAN: 3 1/8–4 inches

HABITAT: Open grassland, swamps, fenland, and damp meadows

RANGE: Across Europe to Asia and Japan; northern Africa; sub-Arctic North America

STATUS: Widespread and common

BLACK SWALLOWTAIL

PAPILIO POLYXENES

A common and widespread swallowtail, the Black Swallowtail, as its name suggests, is mainly black. It has a bright yellow band across both wings; yellow spots also line the margins of both wings. Females often show less yellow than the males with a narrower band. Both have an iridescent blue patch on each hindwing between the bands. It has a small red eyespot on the inner edge of each hindwing and its abdomen is black lined with yellow spots. Can usually be seen flying in the full sun, looking for flowers to feed on.

CATERPILLAR: Bright green with black stripes spotted with red. Feeds on carrot, milkweed, dill, and fennel
WINGSPAN: 3¹⁄₈–4 inches
HABITAT: Open grassland, swamps, fenland, and damp meadows
RANGE: Across Europe to Asia and Japan; northern Africa, sub-Arctic North America
STATUS: Widespread and common

APOLLO PARNASSIUS APOLLO

CATERPILLAR: Black with orange side spots. Feeds on sedum and houseleek

WINGSPAN: 2³/₈–4 inches

HABITAT: Alpine meadows and mountain slopes; in the colder northern part of its range it keeps to lower altitudes

RANGE: European and Central Asian mountain ranges

STATUS: Generally common but highly sought after by collectors, therefore a protected species

This mountain butterfly is appropriately named after the mountain of the Greek gods, Parnassus. It has a white background color and the forewings are edged with an iridescent gray. The forewings are marked with large black spots and the hindwings bear color spots that can vary from red to orange and dark yellow. These distinctive spots distinguish the Apollo from similar species, such a the Small Apollo, which has a red spot on its forewing, or the Clouded Apollo, which bears no colored spots. The abdomen of the Apollo is covered with relatively long gray hairs and its gray antennae have a black club.

ZERYNTHIA POLYXENA SOUTHERN FESTOON

This striking butterfly has delicate and intricate patterning, making it very distinctive. Its background color is a creamy yellow and this is marked with a variable patterning of almost geometric black markings. The wing-edges are striped with black and cream crescents. It has a red patch on the leading edge of the forewing and several red spots on the hindwing. The Southern Festoon closely resembles the Spanish Festoon (*Zerynthia rumina*) which is more yellow and has a greater number of red patches on the forewing.

CATERPILLAR: Feeds on vines and birthwort

WINGSPAN: 2–2³/₈ inches

HABITAT: Open grassland, agricultural land, and vineyards

RANGE: Central and southern Europe across to Eurasia

STATUS: Common in localized areas; however its habitat is under threat in some places

PIERIDAE
WHITES AND SULFURS

BLACK-VEINED WHITE APORIA CRATAEGI

CATERPILLAR: Hairy gray body with a black back marked with red. Feeds on hawthorns and fruit trees such as peach, apple, and pear

WINGSPAN: $2^3/_8$–$3^1/_8$ inches

HABITAT: Flowery meadows and roadsides, orchards and forest edges

RANGE: Across Europe, although extinct in Britain. Found in north Africa and Asia

STATUS: Common, particularly in orchards, where the larvae are considered pests

A striking white, the black veining on this butterfly makes it distinctive and easy to identify. Its white wings are almost translucent and the veins can appear dark brown to black. It has rounded wings and a large dark gray body with clubbed antennae. The edges of its wings are delicately lined with black; often gray scaling can be seen on the wing-edges and the underside, otherwise the upper side and underside are similar. Large numbers of these butterflies can often be observed together as they drink from puddles. As caterpillars they live communally in the cocoon.

LEPTIDEA SINAPIS WOOD WHITE

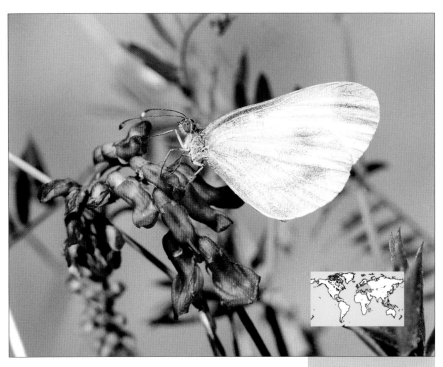

The Wood White is a small, delicate butterfly, with relatively broad rounded wings and a long, slender abdomen. It is a weak flier, often fluttering close to the ground and generally unable to tolerate winds; as a consequence it is usually observed fluttering through foliage rather than above. Its wings are pure white above, with a pale gray coloration at the outer tip of the forewing, a marking that is more pronounced in males. Its white underwing is slightly more yellow, with pale gray streaks along the veins. Its abdomen is gray.

CATERPILLAR: Pale green with a black back and yellow side stripes. Feeds on members of the pea family

WINGSPAN: 1½–2 inches

HABITAT: Mainly woodland, particularly sheltered areas

RANGE: Across Europe, from the British Isles into central Europe

STATUS: Restricted to areas with suitable habitat

LARGE WHITE/ CABBAGE WHITE

PIERIS BRASSICAE

Commonly known as the Large Cabbage White, this common visitor to yards can be distinguished from its smaller relative *Pieris rapae* by its slightly larger size and darker markings. Its wings are predominantly white on the upper side, with two dark spots and black tips on the leading edges of the forewings, markings that are generally darker on the female. Its underside is a greenish yellow with a white central patch on the forewing marked with a black spot. The butterfly is attracted to flowers, but its caterpillar is more infamous as a voracious eater of all members of the cabbage or brassica family.

CATERPILLAR: Green body with a black back bordered with yellow stripes. Feeds on cabbage, but also nasturtiums
WINGSPAN: $2^3/_8$ inches
HABITAT: Meadows, agricultural land, parks, and gardens
RANGE: Widespread across Europe into north Africa
STATUS: Common. Has been known to migrate into northern reaches of its range

GREEN VEINED WHITE PIERIS NAPI

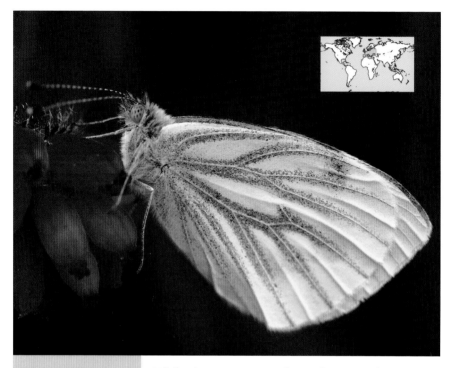

CATERPILLAR: Bright green with fine yellow spots along the sides. Feeds on cress, mustard garlic, and watercress
WINGSPAN: 2 inches
HABITAT: Damp meadows and woodland, yards, and roadside edges
RANGE: Widespread across Europe, from Scandinavia toward the Mediterranean
STATUS: Common

Whilst this may appear to be similar to its relatives the Small and Large Cabbage Whites, the Green-Veined White is most easily distinguished by its veining, particularly on its underwings. It has a background color of white on its upper side, with gray-green veining and either one (males) or two (females) similarly colored spots on the forewing. The forewing tip is marked with dark gray. On its underside the background color is a creamy yellow and on the hindwing this is delicately patterned with gray-green veins. The underside of the forewing is more white but with a yellow tip, and the spots seen on the upperwing are repeated below.

PIERIS RAPAE SMALL WHITE

Like its close relative the *Pieris brassicae*, the Small White is best known for its caterpillars' attraction to cabbage, earning it the common name Small Cabbage White. It is particularly common and easily seen in almost every yard where flowering plants grow. Its upper side is mainly white, with dark gray edges to the tips of the forewings and and one gray spot on males, two on females. The hindwings are creamy white and also bear a gray spot, usually less distinct in males. The underside is a grayish yellow, with a whiter forewing but otherwise matching markings. Small whites are migratory and can often be observed in large groups or swarms.

CATERPILLAR: Small and pale green. Feeds on cabbage, radishes, and nasturtiums

WINGSPAN: 1½–2 inches

HABITAT: Yards, roadsides, meadows, uncultivated fields, and argricultural land

RANGE: This is a widespread butterfly found in most suitable habitats around the world

STATUS: Extremely numerous and common

BATH WHITE

PONTIA DAPLIDICE

This strong, fast flier is a regular migrant and consequently covers a large range. Its background color is white and on the upper side its wings are strongly marked with dark gray, almost black, patterning. On the forewing this is restricted to marks on the outer tip and a large squarish spot in the center, whereas on the hindwing the spots are extensive, producing a marbled effect. From below, the same markings are repeated but in an olive green rather than black. This coloring helps to provide better camouflage when the butterfly is at rest within foliage. Females are slightly larger, with more marbling on the hindwing.

CATERPILLAR: Slender with a green body covered with black spots and yellow stripes along back and sides. Feeds on reseda and rock cress

WINGSPAN: 2 inches

HABITAT: Open, flowery grassland and meadows, roadsides, yards, and parkland

RANGE: Across central and southern Europe, toward north Africa

STATUS: Particularly common toward the southern end of its range

ORANGE SULFUR
COLIAS EURYTHEME

CATERPILLAR: Dark green body with white, black, and pink side stripes. Feeds on alfafa, clover, and other legumes
WINGSPAN: 1½–2⅜ inches
HABITAT: Open fields, agricultural land, meadows, and prairies
RANGE: Across North America
STATUS: More common in south and west; caterpillar is considered a pest in some areas

Found across North America, this species is commonly referred to as the Orange Sulfur, the Alfafa Caterpillar Butterfly or the Alfafa Sulfur. Its background color can vary from bright yellow to a more orange color; yellow examples can usually be seen during spring. Both males and females have a dark brown border across both wings. However, in the female this is incomplete, with patches of the background color showing through. There is a black spot in the center of the forewing, visible from below as a pale spot. An orange spot on the upper side of the hindwing is an identifying feature; this too is pale underneath. The background color on the underside is yellow-green with a row of dark spots at the outer edge of each wing.

CLOUDED/COMMON SULFUR
COLIAS PHILODICE

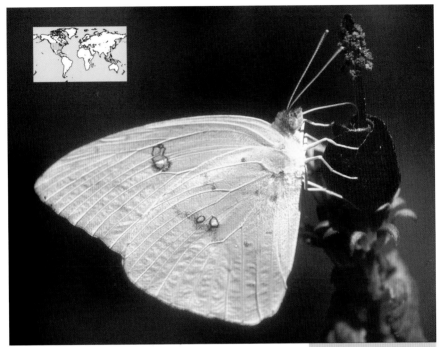

This common North American butterfly can display either clear yellow or yellow-white wings, but generally paler examples are females. Both males and females bear distinctive black outer margins on both wings and in the females this can be broken up with patches of the background wing color. There is a single dark eyespot on the forewing and a single, paler brown spot on the hindwing. These markings show through on the solid-colored underside, with the hindwing spot showing as white edged with black.

CATERPILLAR: Green and white striped body. Feeds on clover and alfalfa
WINGSPAN: 2–2¾ inches
HABITAT: Open fields and agricultural land, roadside edges
RANGE: Across North America
STATUS: Generally common

CLOUDED YELLOW

COLIAS CROCEA

A native of southern Europe, this fast-flying butterfly is able to migrate long distances toward the north, extending its range substantially. The males are brighter than the females, with an upperwing background color of orange-yellow broadly bordered with dark brown. The forewing bears a dark brown spot in its center. On its underwing the male has an orange-yellow background color with a green tinge to the forewing margin and the hindwing. It shows a dark spot on the forewing and a pale, ringed spot on the hindwing. Females are much less vivid and generally a more greenish yellow.

CATERPILLAR: Slender and pale green with white side stripes delicately spotted with red. Feeds on clover and sweet-peas
WINGSPAN: 2 inches
HABITAT: Open grassland, meadows, agricultural land, and wasteland
RANGE: Southern and central Europe, reaching as far north as Britain
STATUS: Common in its native habitat, less so further north

PALE CLOUDED YELLOW COLIAS HYALE

CATERPILLAR: Pale green with a white stripe along the side. Feeds on clover and alfalfa

WINGSPAN: 2 inches

HABITA: Open lowland, particularly flowery grassland, meadows, and agricultural fields

RANGE: Northern and central Europe

STATUS: Generally common in its range

This is similar in appearance to its relative the Clouded Yellow, but as its name suggests it is paler and shows no orange; this is the most usual feature by which to differentiate the two. The Pale Clouded Yellow also has a slightly more pointed forewing. Females are much paler than the males, but both are yellow, the males more vividly so. The forewing bears a central black spot and the hindwing has a pale spot ringed with reddish brown. The female's forewing is almost white, particularly from the underside. When at rest, it keeps its wings closed above its body.

GONEPTERYX CLEOPATRA CLEOPATRA

Similar in appearance to its relative the Brimstone, the Cleopatra inhabits a more southerly range and has more strikingly colored upper wings. It is predominantly bright yellow above, with the center of the forewing showing bright orange in the males. The hindwing bears a small orange-brown spot. Females are generally much paler. The underside is a pale green-yellow with a small ruddy brown spot in the center of each wing. Its most distinguishing feature is the orange streak across the center of the forewing on the underside. Again, females are much paler below, being almost white in color. Both sexes have hooked forewing tips and angular hindwings, giving them a leaf-like appearance when at rest.

CATERPILLAR: Pale green with a fine white stripe along the sides. Feeds on buckthorn.

WINGSPAN: $2^3/_8$–$2^3/_4$ inches

HABITAT: Woodland edges, scrubland, open and lightly wooded lowland

RANGE: Mediterranean Europe down to north Africa

STATUS: Common in its chosen habitat

BRIMSTONE

GONEPTERYX RHAMNI

Aside from its interesting appearance, the Brimstone is also the butterfly credited with the invention of the common English term for all Lepidoptera: its yellow coloring originally earning it the name "butter-colored fly." It is only the male Brimstone that is yellow on its upper side, however: females are a creamy white color. On the underside, the male is a yellow-green shade and when its wings are folded at rest it takes on the appearance of a fresh leaf. Again the female is far paler on the underside; however, both bear a small brown spot on each wing. The hooked tip of the forewing and the angular shape of the hindwing contribute to its leaf-like appearance.

CATERPILLAR: Slender and pale green with a fine white stripe along the side. Feeds on buckthorn
WINGSPAN: 2³⁄₈ inches
HABITAT: Woodland edges, flowery grassland, meadows, yards, and fenland
RANGE: Europe, from Britain down toward the Mediterranean
STATUS: Generally common

ORANGE TIP

ANTHOCHARIS CARDAMINES

Males and females in this species are quite different, with the striking males being the most easily recognized of the two. Both are white butterflies; however the male has a bright orange tip to the forewing which is edged with brown and bears a small brown central spot. The female has no orange, but a broader brown tip and a larger central spot on the forewing. Both have delicate, olive-green mottled hindwings on the underside, which helps to provide camouflage when the butterfly is at rest. Females are very similar to the slightly darker female Bath Whites, and consequently difficult to identify.

CATERPILLAR: Pale gray-green with white side stripes. Feeds on *Cardamine pratensis* and garlic mustard
WINGSPAN: 1 1/2–2 inches
HABITAT: Light woodland, meadows and grassland, fenland and sometimes yards
RANGE: Across Europe toward Asia
STATUS: Common

TIGER PIERID

DISMORPHIA AMPHIONE

Although this is a Pierid butterfly, the Tiger Pierid has an unusually long and narrow wing shape that more closely resembles that of the *Heliconius* butterflies. It is an effective mimic, with striking black, orange and yellow wings that suggest poisons to potential predators. The pattern of its markings can vary, but generally the forewing is backgrounded in black with orange patches from the base and yellow patches toward the tip. The dark hindwing has a large orange patch on females, and an orange streak accompanied by a translucent white patch on males.

CATERPILLAR: Dark green body. Feeds on *Inga sapindoides*
WINGSPAN: $1\frac{1}{2}$–$1\frac{3}{4}$ inches
HABITAT: Tropical forests
RANGE: South and central America, West Indies
STATUS: Generally common

ORANGE-BARRED GIANT SULFUR

PHOEBIS PHILEA

As its common name suggests, this is a large sulfur with broad wings clearly marked with orange. The sexes are slightly different: males have shallower wings, which are solid yellow with a distinctive orange patch or bar on the forewing. The female has squared wings, also yellow but with dark brown edges and spotting on the forewing and a red blush to the edges of the hindwing. This red coloring includes a row of red-brown oval spots along the edge. From underneath, both sexes are a solid orange-yellow, darker in the female, and both show a dark-ringed white spot in the center of each wing.

CATERPILLAR: Pale green body with brown side stripe. Feeds on senna
WINGSPAN: 2¾–3 inches
HABITAT: Subtropical forest edges and clearings
RANGE: Southern states of the USA into Central America toward southern Brazil
STATUS: Generally common

LYCENIDAE
GOSSAMER WINGS

GREEN HAIRSTREAK CALLOPHRYS RUBI

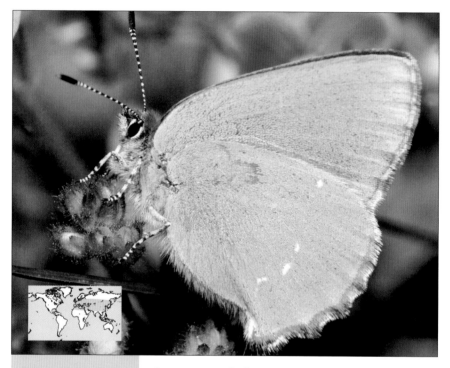

CATERPILLAR: Green body with dark back and diagonal yellow stripes. Feeds on low-growing plants such as gorse and heather

WINGSPAN: 1 inch

HABITAT: Scrubland, heaths, meadows, open grassland, and woodland edges

RANGE: Across Europe into Asia and north Africa

STATUS: Generally common

On its upper side the Green Hairstreak is a fairly dull brown color; its veins are slightly darker than the background shade, and males show a small pale scent patch near the leading edge of the forewing. It is the underside of the butterfly that earns it the common name, as both wings are a bright, leafy green. On the hindwing there is a broken white band, which continues on to the forewing, but only faintly. Its slightly scalloped hindwing is fringed with white and brown. When at rest, the Green Hairstreak keeps its wings closed, making it extremely difficult to spot in foliage.

EUMAEUS ATALA ATALA

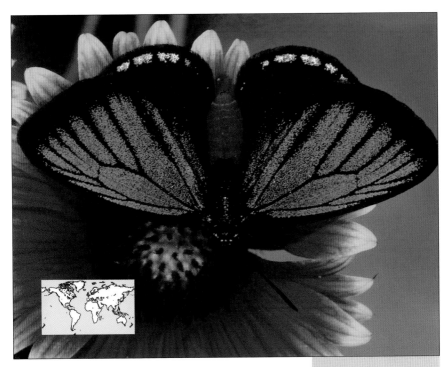

Although considered a hairstreak, the Atala lacks any tails, nor indeed are its hindwings scalloped. It is a striking butterfly, with black wings washed with iridescent blue-green scales. The hindwing bears a single row of metallic-blue spots along the marginal edge on the upper side, and from below there are three rows of the same markings. The bright red abdomen and red hindwing spot are distinctive and enable identification. The thorax and head of the butterfly are black with faint blue spotting. Virtually extinct in the United States, the Atala has been successfully reintroduced.

CATERPILLAR: Red body with yellow spotting. Feeds on zamia

WINGSPAN: 1½–2 inches

HABITAT: Tropical and subtropical forests, parks and yards

RANGE: Central America, Cuba, the Bahamas into Florida

STATUS: Increasingly common

PURPLE HAIRSTREAK

QUERCUSIA QUERCUS

When at rest, this hairstreak will sometimes leave its wings open, allowing observers to identify it by the markings on its upperwings. These have a sooty brown background color with bright patches of iridescent purple. On the male, the purple covers almost all of both wings, leaving the brown at the outer margins, whereas the females show purple only on a patch at the center of the forewing. The underside of both sexes is a pale silvery gray with a single white streak along the outer edge and small orange spots on the tip of the hindwing. There is a very small tail on the hindwing.

CATERPILLAR: Ruddy brown body with dark brown markings. Feeds on oak trees
WINGSPAN: ¾–1¼ inches
HABITAT: Mainly deciduous woodland, particulary those containing oak
RANGE: Across Europe into Asia and toward north Africa
STATUS: Generally common

GRAY HAIRSTREAK
STRYMON MELINUS

CATERPILLAR: Green with white markings along its side. Feeds on a variey of plants, including cotton, maize, and hops, resulting in its being considered a pest

WINGSPAN: $3/4$–$1\frac{1}{4}$ inches

HABITAT: Open land, fields, meadows, yards, roadside verges and forest edges.

RANGE: From Canada, through to Central and South America

STATUS: Widespread and very common

This is one of the most common and widespread hairstreaks in North America. The larva of the Gray Hairstreak feeds on a wide variety of plants, allowing it to prosper in a range of habitats. From above the male is dark gray and bears an orange and black eyespot above the tail on the hindwing. Females are a more brownish gray. On its underside, this species is silvery gray with a delicate orange, black, and white band crossing the wings. Its orange and black eyespot can be seen from the underside. Its body and abdomen correspond with the wing coloration, dark above, paler below.

WHITE LETTER HAIRSTREAK
STRYMONIDIA W-ALBUM

At first glance this is simply a dull brown hairstreak, but the white markings on both underside wings are distinctive and enable a clear identification. From above it has dark, chocolate-brown wings with gentle scalloping and two short tails on the hindwing. On the underside the wings are a slightly paler brown, with a clear W-shaped white streak across both wings. At the outer margin of the hindwing are a number of crescent-shaped orange patches forming a bright band. The upper side of the wings is rarely seen when the butterfly is at rest.

CATERPILLAR: Pale green body with pinkish diagonal streaks and dark green back stripes. Feeds on elm

WINGSPAN: $1\frac{1}{8}$–$1\frac{1}{2}$ inches

HABITAT: Deciduous woodland, woodland edges, and hedgerows

RANGE: Across Europe into Asia

STATUS: Generally common, but numbers affected by Dutch elm disease

BROWN HAIRSTREAK THECLA BETULAE

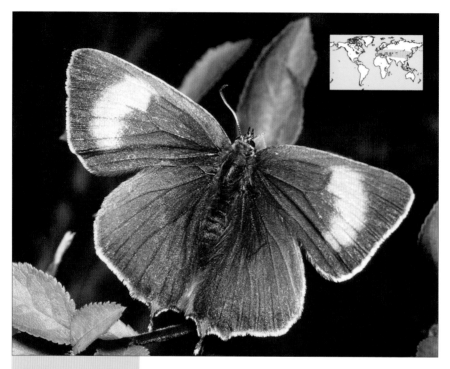

CATERPILLAR: Green with yellow stripes. Feeds on blackthorn

WINGSPAN: 1 $\frac{1}{8}$–1 $\frac{1}{2}$ inches

HABITAT: Woodland edges, hedgerows, and scrubland

RANGE: Across Europe into Asia

STATUS: Relatively common within chosen habitat, where small colonies are formed

From above, as its names suggests, the Brown Hairstreak is mainly brown in color, with orange patches on the forewing which are larger in the female than the male. Both sexes also bear an orange mark on the small tail. From below the Brown Hairstreak is more remarkable, with a subtle orange background color marked with two delicate black and white lines on each wing. The tail streamer is a brighter orange from below. Its body shows dark brown from above and paler below.

LYCAENA DISPAR LARGE COPPER

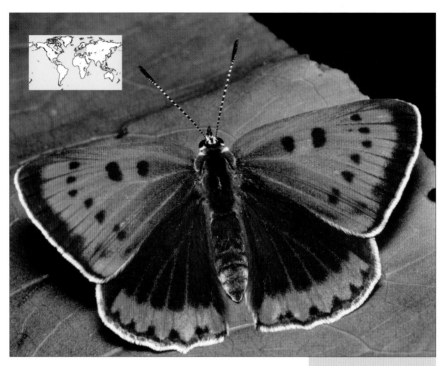

Despite its small size, the Large Copper is relatively big in comparison to other coppers. Males have upperwings that are a bright coppery orange, clearly bordered with dark brown and bearing a small brown spot in the center of the forewing. Females are less bright, with a greater amount of dark brown, a broader brown border on the forewing and dull brown hindwings; they also bear a number of brown spots along the length of the forewing. On the underside, the sexes are similar, with an orange forewing bearing dark spots and a bright, blue-gray hindwing with black spots and an orange band.

CATERPILLAR: Bright green with raised white spots. Feeds on water dock and varieties of aquatic sorrel

WINGSPAN: 1 $\frac{1}{8}$–1 $\frac{1}{2}$ inches

HABITAT: Damp grassland, marshes, fenland, and the banks of slow-flowing rivers

RANGE: Localized from eastern Britain, into northern and central Europe.

STATUS: Numbers are in decline due to degradation of habitat

SMALL COPPER

LYCAENA PHLAEAS

This species of copper has a wide range, mainly thanks to its host plant, sorrel, which grows in abundance in the warm and temperate parts of the globe. Males and females are similar, with bright orange forewings bordered with brown and bearing black spots. The hindwings are grayish brown with an orange border marked with brown spots. The underwings are similarly marked but the colors are less bright. It has a dark body and long antennae ringed in black and white.

CATERPILLAR: Green with purple and pink markings. Feeds on sorrel and dock
WINGSPAN: $3/4$–$1 1/4$ inches
HABITAT: Open grassland, fields, meadows, and roadsides
RANGE: Found across temperate Northern Hemisphere
STATUS: Widespread and extremely common

SOOTY COPPER LYCAENA TITYRUS

CATERPILLAR: Plump, green body. Feeds on dock and sorrel
WINGSPAN: 1–1½ inches
HABITAT: Open grassland, flowery meadows, low-lying mountain slopes, and coastal fields
RANGE: Across Europe but not Britain or Scandinavia
STATUS: Generally common

It is the male that is more "sooty" in appearance, with upperwings that are a dark blackish brown with black spots on both wings. On the hindwing marginal edge there is a series of orange spots making an irregular line. The female is slightly more colorful, with orange forewings marked with black spots and a much more defined orange band around the hindwing edge. From below its wings are a paler gray, with the black markings showing through and a row of orange spots along the edge of both wings.

ARICIA AGESTIS BROWN ARGUS

This attractive little brown butterfly can be identified by the distinctive orange spots along its wing margins. Its upperwings are a rich brown color and the bright orange spots are highlighted with black on the hindwings. The forewing has a single black spot at its center. The slightly larger females have proportionally bigger spot markings. From underneath, the pale gray-brown wings are marked with white-ringed black spots. The orange spots are repeated from the upper side, with the black highlights on the hindwing ringed in white. In addition, a white streak marks the center of the hindwing. The white wing fringe is visible on both sides.

CATERPILLAR: Green body with purple and dark green stripes. Feeds on rock rose and cranesbill
WINGSPAN: 1 inch
HABITAT: Open grassland and heaths
RANGE: Temperate northern Europe
STATUS: Generally common

HOLLY BLUE CELASTRINA ARGIOLUS

CATERPILLAR: Pale green with pink stripes along the sides and back. Feeds on holly and ivy
WINGSPAN: $^3/_3$–$1^1/_4$ inches
HABITAT: Mainly woodland but also parks and yards, wherever host plants can be found
RANGE: Across Europe, down to north Africa and through to Asia
STATUS: Generally common and widespread

A fairly frequent visitor to yards, the Holly Blue is an easily identified member of the blues. It is particularly attracted to those yards where holly and ivy are grown, since it uses both these plants to host its larva. Both males and females have blue upperwings; however the female is more pale and dull and shows a greater amount of brownish black on the wing margins. The male is a bright violet blue, with a narrow black margin at the forewing tip. Both have a short white fringe which is intermittently marked with black. The pale silvery-blue underwings are marked with small black spots.

EVERES COMYNTAS EASTERN TAILED BLUE

This species of common blue has, as its name suggests, a fine hair-like tail on its hindwings. In coloration males and females differ: males are deep blue from above with a narrow black border; females are a dark gray, often shot with blue. Both sexes bear a pair of orange and black eyespots on the tail end of the hindwing. From below, both are a dirty white marked with dark gray spots in a curving line. The eyespots are visible on the underwing.

CATERPILLAR: Green with brown and paler green stripes. Feeds on clover

WINGSPAN: ³/₄ inch

HABITAT: Open grassland, meadows, fields, roadsides and large yards

RANGE: South-eastern Canada, eastern states of North America into Central America

STATUS: Common

LONG-TAILED BLUE LAMPIDES BOETICUS

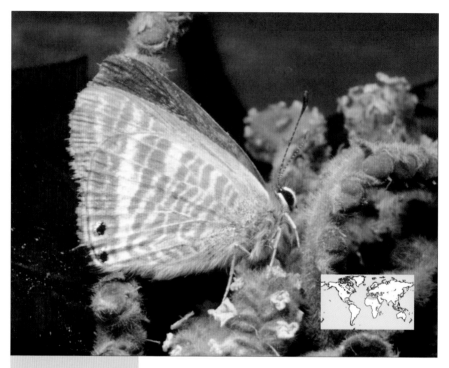

CATERPILLAR: Pale green body with darker green back stripe, and pale diagonal stripes. Feeds on pea plants
WINGSPAN: 1¼ inches
HABITAT: Open grassland, meadows, heathland
RANGE: Mediterranean Europe into north Africa
STATUS: Generally common within its native range

This migratory butterfly is native to the south of Europe, but will often succeed in making its way as far north as southern England. It has fairly pointed forewings and squarer hindwings with a distinctive tail, not dissimilar to that of a typical hairstreak. However, the Long-tailed Blue's coloring is distinctive. Males are a solid violet-blue on the upper side with a white patch bearing two black eyespots above the tail; females are more brown from above, with violet-blue showing at the base of the wings. From below, both sexes are much paler brown, with buff and white streaks and bars across both wings and the eyespots boldly repeated.

MACULINEA ARION LARGE BLUE

As a member of the Maculinea genus, the Large Blue's caterpillars rely upon the eggs of red ants in order to pupate. Young caterpillars allow themselves to be carried into the nest by the ants; they then gorge themselves on the grubs, leaving the nest after pupation as a fresh butterfly. Males and females are both blue from above, although the female shows deep brown wing margins. Both sexes bear black marks on the upper forewing. The underside is a gray-brown patterned with brown spots ringed with white. Females tend to be slightly larger than males.

CATERPILLAR: Creamy white body. Feeds on thyme and marjoram plants then ant eggs and larvae

WINGSPAN: 1–1½ inches

HABITAT: Dry, chalky grassland, wherever caterpillar food sources are present

RANGE: Europe, excluding Britain, into Asia and China

STATUS: Widespread but scarce and declining

ADONIS BLUE

LYSANDRA BELLARGUS

The males of the Adonis Blue species are a particularly striking bright blue color from above, and their wings are fringed with a white and black checkered border. The female is a rich brown color above, with blue scales producing a subtle sheen. At the base of the female's hindwings there is a border of crescent-shaped orange spots. Both sexes have gray-brown underwings which are marked with black spots and a border of orange and black on each wing.

CATERPILLAR: Green body with yellow stripes. Feeds on horseshoe vetch
WINGSPAN: 1–1 ½ inches
HABITAT: Dry, open grassland and meadows
RANGE: From western Europe into Asia
STATUS: Generally common, but numbers slowly being affected by habitat loss

ACMON BLUE PLEBEJUS ACMON

CATERPILLAR: Yellow-green body with dark green back stripe and white hairs. Feeds on legumes and buckwheat foliage
WINGSPAN: 1 inch
HABITAT: Open, dry fields, wasteland, agricultural land, meadows
RANGE: Across North America, from southern Canada toward Mexico
STATUS: Generally common

This North American blue can most easily be identified by the band of orange spots that lines the hindwing. As is typical, it is the male butterfly that is blue on the upper side; the female is a rich brown color with the merest suggestion of blue at the wing base. The edges of both wings are dark blue-black, which contrasts strongly with the white fringe. The hindwing spots are black on a base of orange. These orange and black spots are repeated on the underside of the wing, which is a pale gray color and which also bears simple black spotting.

PLEBEJUS ARGUS SILVER STUDDED BLUE

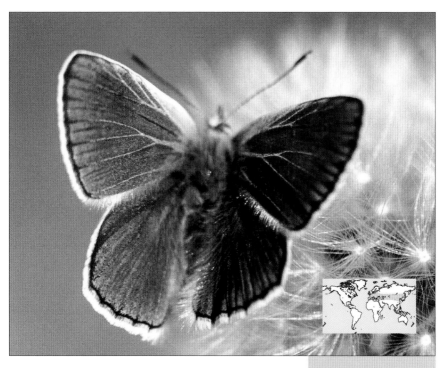

This is a particularly active and fast-flying blue, which tends to rest only early or late in the day. Males are a deep azure blue bordered with brown and then deep white wing-edges and fringe. The upperwings of the female are mainly brown with a crescent of orange marginal spots on the hindwing. Both sexes have pale gray underwings, which are marked with black spots, those on the hindwing having a slightly green hue. Both underwings bear a marginal line of orange spots. Its hairy body is blue-gray above and paler below.

CATERPILLAR: Green body with white side stripes and a black back. Feeds on heather and gorse. In some areas the larvae pupate inside ants' nests

WINGSPAN: $^3/_4$–$1^1/_8$ inches

HABITAT: Heathland, hillside meadows, low mountain grassland, and dunes

RANGE: Across Europe into Asia toward Japan

STATUS: Common and widespread

IDAS BLUE

PLEBEJUS IDAS

A small, attractive blue with dissimilar males and females. Typical males have violet-blue upperwings with a fine black margin and a hairy white fringe. The upperwing of the female is a rich brown color. Their underwings are similar, with a background color of pale gray-brown marked with black spots and an orange band of spots curving parallel to the outer margins.

CATERPILLAR: Pale green back bordered with white stripes and black sides. Feeds on members of the pea family
WINGSPAN: 1 inch
HABITAT: Open grassland, meadows, fields, and agricultural land
RANGE: Across northern and central Europe, including higher altitudes
STATUS: Common

COMMON BLUE
POLYOMMATUS ICARUS

CATERPILLAR: Green body with pale green markings. Feeds on bird's-foot trefoil
WINGSPAN: 1⅛–1½ inches
HABITAT: Open grassland, including higher altitude meadows
RANGE: Across Europe into Asia and north Africa
STATUS: Widespread and common

A typical blue butterfly, the Common Blue is also, as its name suggests, the blue butterfly most often observed in the field. The male has bright violet-blue upperwings with a delicate brown border and white fringe along the outer edges. The female has upperwings that are a solid rich brown color with orange spots and crescents along the outer margins of both wings. Across some areas females will also show a blue wash to the inner base of the wings. Both sexes have similar undersides, which are pale gray-brown marked with black white-ringed spots and a marginal border of orange spots.

DUKE OF BURGUNDY FRITILLARY
HAMEARIS LUCINA

Although its name suggests otherwise, the Duke of Burgundy belongs not to the Nymphalidae species of fritillaries, but to the Riodinidae. It is the only metalmark butterfly native to Europe, and although it bears a strong resemblance to other fritillaries its behavior is closer to that of the blues. From above, its deep brown wings are marked with a checkered pattern of orange spots and its fringe is checkered white and brown. It is orange-brown below, with dark spots on the forewing and broad white markings on the hindwing. The sexes are generally alike, but the female is slightly brighter and has more rounded forewings.

CATERPILLAR: Brown body with a dark stripe along the back. Feeds on primrose and cowslip
WINGSPAN: 1 1/8–1 1/2 inches
HABITAT: Woodland edges, meadows and gardens
RANGE: Western and central Europe
STATUS: Generally common in local areas

NYMPHALIDAE
BRUSHFOOTS

WHITE PEACOCK

ANARTIA JATROPHAE

A common butterfly to Central and South America and the West Indies, the White Peacock is an attractive gray-white color marked with bands of brown which create a checkered pattern. The wing margins are bordered with brown-orange crescents and the wings are gently scalloped, more so on the hindwing, which has a short tail. There are two dark eyespots on the hindwing and one on the forewing, and these are visible from below. The underside is much paler, showing more white, but with the pattern reproduced in pale orange and brown. Males and females are similar.

CATERPILLAR: Black body with black spines and silver spots. Feeds on water hyssop
WINGSPAN: 2–2³/₈ inches
HABITAT: Open land, fields, wasteland, yards, and roadsides
RANGE: Central and South America, West Indies, and southern states of North America
STATUS: Common and widespread

PURPLE EMPEROR APATURA IRIS

CATERPILLAR: Plump, pale green body. Feeds on willow

WINGSPAN: $2^{3}/_{8}$–3 inches

HABITAT: Deciduous woodland, particularly those with mature oaks, the tops of which are the preferred territory for males

RANGE: From western Europe into central Asia

STATUS: Generally common, but difficult to observe in the forest canopy

At first sight a Purple Emperor may not appear to be purple at all; it is only when caught in the right light that males flash their colors. Males and females bear similar markings and both appear to have a background color of brown on their upperwings. However, males have wing scales that are sensitive to light, producing bright purple. This is bordered on both wings with blackish brown and marked with a white bar across the hindwing which breaks up into spots on the forewing. There is a large purple, black and orange spot on the hindwing. From below both sexes are brown with white patches on both wings and a large purple, black and orange eyespot on the forewing. The smaller spot on the hindwing shows through on the underwing.

ASTEROCAMPA CELTIS HACKBERRY BUTTERFLY

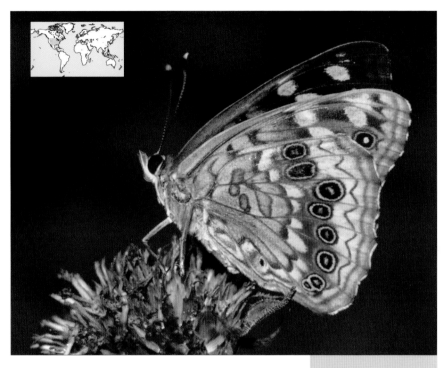

It is the caterpillar of this species which feeds upon hackberry bushes; the butterfly can more usually be seen feeding from tree sap or animal droppings. The Hackberry Butterfly has tawny-brown wings with white spotting on the forewing tips and dark spots on the hindwing. The upper side of the forewing has a distinctive black spot on the outer edge and there is a series of black spots along the margin of the hindwing. From underneath the Hackberry has a paler background color, with similar white-ringed eyespotting on the hindwing.

CATERPILLAR: Green body with yellow stripes. Feeds on hackberry

WINGSPAN: 1½–2¼ inches

HABITAT: A variety, including river woodland, desert canyon, and urban parks

RANGE: Across North America

STATUS: Widespread and common

THE VICEROY

BASILARCHIA ARCHIPPUS

The Viceroy is an effective mimic of the more poisonous Monarch butterfly. Although it is edible for predators, it is still a successfully common and widespread butterfly across North America. Like the Monarch's, its upperwings have a background color of orange which is boldly patterned with black wing veins and black borders marked with small white spots. However, it has an additional black line running across its hindwing, a feature that is repeated on its underside. From below its wings are paler; the hindwing has a background color of pale, pinkish orange and the forewing is pale orange with a central darker orange patch.

Caterpillar: Olive-green and brown body with bristles behind the head. Feeds on decidous trees, particularly willow
Wingspan: 2¾–3 inches
Habitat: Open, damp areas, river edges, streams, marshes
Range: Widespread from Canada down into Mexico
Status: Generally common

RED LACEWING

CETHOSIA BIBLIS

The Latin name for the Red Lacewing reflects the patterning on the underside of the wings, which can look like writing in a book (*biblios*). This poisonous butterfly has a background color of rich ruddy brown below, with a delicate pattern of white and black lines. From above, males and females are different: the males are brighter, with an orange-red background color, broad brown borders on the outer wing-edges, and white V-shaped markings along the margins. Females are either much more brown above, or an olive-green color, with similar white markings. Both sexes have scalloped wings.

CATERPILLAR: Poisonous spined body. Feeds on passionflowers
WINGSPAN: $3\frac{1}{8}$–$3\frac{1}{2}$ inches
HABITAT: Forest edges and clearings
RANGE: India and Pakistan across to China, Malaysia, and Indonesia
STATUS: Generally common

OWL BUTTERFLY CALIGO IDOMENEUS

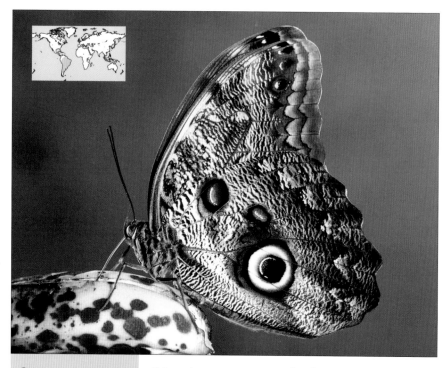

CATERPILLAR: Brown body with a forked tail. Feeds on banana leaves and is considered a pest on plantations
WINGSPAN: 4¾–6 inches
HABITAT: Tropical forests and suitable agricultural land
RANGE: Found throughout South America
STATUS: Common and widespread

Caligo idomeneus is an example of a genus of South American butterflies which are large and marked with enormous owl-like eyespots. Its upper side is a rich dark brown shot through with purple-blue iridescence. There is a white diagonal line running down the forewing which diffuses into pale blue on the darker brown hindwing. The underside is patterned with fine brown and white feathered lines and the forewing edge has a slender brown border. There are two small eyespots in the outer tip of the forewing but the hindwing is marked with two larger eyespots, that in the center of the hindwing being bigger and more startling for potential predators. Although diurnal, these butterflies, like owls, fly during the early hours and at dusk.

CHARAXES JASIUS TWO-TAILED PASHA

The Two-tailed Pasha is the only double-tailed butterfly found in Europe. It has angular wings with gently scalloped hindwings leading to two significant tails. On the upper side the wings are brown, with pale orange borders and subtle blue spots at the base of the tails. On its underside there is a delicate and intricate pattern of white lines with a broad white band running down both fore- and hindwing. Between the white lines it is colored with black, brown, orange, and purple-gray. It is also distinguished by being one of the largest members of the Nympalidae family, and by its tendency to gorge itself on the juice of rotten fruit, rendering it too intoxicated to fly.

CATERPILLAR: Green with white spots. Feeds on strawberry trees
WINGSPAN: $2^3/_4$–$3^1/_8$ inches
HABITAT: Orchards, woodland and forests, scrubland
RANGE: Mediterranean Europe down toward north Africa
STATUS: Generally locally common

PAINTED LADY

CYNTHIA CARDUI

This is a strong migratory butterfly, whose caterpillars are content to consume a wide variety of plants; consequently it can successfully survive almost anywhere. Its upperwings are patterned with orange and black, with white spots on the the forewing. The gentle scalloped hindwings are edged with black and there are four black spots lining the outer margin. On the underside it is much paler, with the forewing repeating the upperside pattern and the hindwing marbled in white-brown and pinks. The four distinguishing spots are repeated below and ringed with orange and black.

CATERPILLAR: Black with white spots and black or yellow spines. Prefers to feed on thistle and nettle, but will eat many other plants
WINGSPAN: 2–2³/₈ inches
HABITAT: Most open land with plentiful flowers. Regularly visits yards
RANGE: Widespread across the world, native to warm southern climes
STATUS: Very common

BALTIMORE CHECKERSPOT

EUPHYDRYAS PHAETON

This largely black butterfly is marked with distinctive white and orange spotting on its upper side, which greatly aids identification. Observation is also helped by the fact that the Baltimore Checkerspot uses the widespread plantain as a larval host plant. From above its black wings are bordered with orange spots, with smaller white spotting toward the center. A pair of orange spots mark the forewing leading edge and a single spot is seen at the center of the hindwing. From below it is marked with black and white checkering, and a less prominent orange band on the outer edges. It is named after the design of the heraldic shield of the first Lord Baltimore, a seventeenth-century colonist.

CATERPILLAR: Black body with orange side stripe and black spines. Feeds on turtlehead, white ash, and plantain
WINGSPAN: 1½–2⅝ inches
HABITAT: Wet meadows and grassland, sphagnum bogs and drier hillsides
RANGE: Throughout eastern states of the US, from Nova Scotia
STATUS: Generally common

PEACOCK INACHIS IO

CATERPILLAR: Black and spiny body. Feeds in large colonies on nettle and hop

WINGSPAN: 2–2³/₈ inches

HABITAT: Grassy meadows, fields and open land, parks, and yards. Particularly attracted to buddleia

RANGE: Across Europe into cooler parts of Asia and Japan

STATUS: Widespread and very common

From below the Peacock is a dull, mottled brown with untidily scalloped wing-edges, which provides good leaf camouflage. On its upperside it is mainly bright red with black edges lined with brown. It has a large eyespot on the tip of the forewing that is red, yellow, and blue ringed with black. There is also a pair of smaller, pure white spots on the outer margins of the forewing. The large eyespot on the hindwing is blue and black ringed with creamy white. On the inner half of the leading edge of the forewing there is a narrow band of fine yellow and black stripes. Birds, confused by the bold eyespots, will often launch a peck at the wings of the Peacock. This has the effect of alerting the butterfly to the danger and tends to leave many of this species with ragged, damaged wings.

JUNONIA COENIA BUCKEYE

Male Buckeyes are notoriously territorial and will patrol their chosen space seeking out both mates and intruders. As a result they cover wide areas, traveling north during the summer months as they look for territory. They are brown-colored from above with a pair of orange bars on the leading edge of the forewing. The most distinctive features are the large black eyespots ringed with orange, white and black—one on the forewing and two on the hindwing. The underside is gray-brown with similar bars but no eyespot.

CATERPILLAR: Dark olive-green with yellow and orange marks. Feeds on plantains
WINGSPAN: 2–2³⁄₈ inches
HABITAT: Open sunny fields, grassland, and shorelines
RANGE: Across North America, from Canada to Mexico
STATUS: Common and widespread

INDIAN LEAF BUTTERFLY

KALLIMA INACHUS

This butterfly earns its common name from the impressive camouflage patterning of its underside and for the shape of its wings, which closely resemble leaves. When at rest its underwings show brown, with paler vein markings and a single white "mold" spot in the center of the forewing. There is a line across both wings that resembles the spine of a leaf, and the hindwing tails closely resemble a leaf's stem. The wings themselves are angular with pointed forewing tips. The upper-side is much brighter: the forewings are broadly striped with brown, orange, and blue, and the hindwings are brown with an iridescent blue wash. The Indian Leaf Butterfly is a particularly strong, rapid flier.

CATERPILLAR: Black body with red spines and yellow hairs. Feeds on girardinia and strobilanthus
WINGSPAN: 3½–4¾ inches
HABITAT: Rainforests, forest riverbanks
RANGE: From India and Pakistan across to China
STATUS: Generally common

WHITE ADMIRAL
LADOGA CAMILLA

CATERPILLAR: Brown body with green back and brown spines which extend on to the head. Feeds on honeysuckle

WINGSPAN: 2–2³⁄₈ inches

HABITAT: Sunny clearings in mature woodland

RANGE: Western Europe, including southern England, across to central Asia and Japan

STATUS: Common, but not always easy to observe

The White Admiral is a rich black color from above with bold white bands crossing the hindwing into the center of the forewing. The forewing also bears large white spots at the outer tip. The round and gently scalloped hindwing is edged with fine crescents of white. All of these white markings are repeated on the underside of the butterfly; however there are additional white and black spots present on both the forewing and the hindwing and all of these are set against a background color of orange-brown. The base of the underside hindwings is blue-gray, which extends into the color of the body and abdomen.

SOUTHERN SNOUT BUTTERFLY
LIBYTHEANA CARINENTA

The Southern or American Snout Butterfly has an unusual appearance on two counts: its forewing tips are squared off, and it has a long "nose" or snout-like protuberance from its face. Its wings from above are a black-brown color with orange patches at the bases and white patches at the forewing tips. From below, its forewings match the upper side, while the hindwings are pale, mottled gray and brown, resembling a dry leaf. This migratory butterfly can appear in huge numbers in the southern part of its range, with swarms often exceeding the million mark.

CATERPILLAR: Dark green body with yellow stripes. Feeds on hackberry

WINGSPAN: 1½–2 inches

HABITAT: Woodland, edges and clearings, open fields, and agricultural land

RANGE: Southern states of the USA into Central America

STATUS: More common in south-western states, generally numerous

BLUE MORPHO

MORPHO MENELAUS

The morphos are a sub-family of beautiful iridescent-blue butterflies that inhabit the rainforests of South America. The Morpho Peleides, commonly known as the Blue Morpho or the Common Morpho, is a striking example. From above it has striking iridescent blue wings broadly edged on the outer margins by deep brown-black. The dark forewing tips bear small white spots and both wings are gently scalloped. From below it is brown-edged with a series of fine white and cream lines. It has large black- and yellow-ringed eyespots, four on the hindwing, three on the fore, and these are used to confuse and deter predators. These strong, fast fliers are attracted to fermenting fruit.

Caterpillar: Striped red, brown, and black with yellow back patches and red and brown hair tufts. When threatened it emits a strong scent. Feeds on pea plants
Wingspan: $3\frac{1}{2}$–$4\frac{3}{4}$ inches
Habitat: Rainforest
Range: Central and South America and the West Indies
Status: Generally common, but threatened by both collectors and habitat loss

MALACHITE METAMORPHA STELENES

CATERPILLAR: Black with red spines. Feeds on ruellia and acanthus
WINGSPAN: 2³⁄₄–3¹⁄₂ inches
HABITAT: Subtropical forests, orchards, low mountain slopes, plantations
RANGE: South and Central America up into Florida, Jamaica and Cuba
STATUS: Very common

The semi-precious mineral malachite is a rich green color, and the Malachite Butterfly has wings that are backgrounded with black and then patterned with bright green or yellowy-green patches. On the upper side, the green markings appear as a broad diagonal band across both wings from the base, with broken patches at the forewing tips. The hindwings, which are scalloped and slightly tailed, have a broken band of green patches along the marginal edge. From below the background color is much paler light brown with olive markings. Females are larger and have paler wings.

NEPTIS SAPPHO COMMON GLIDER

The Common Glider earns it name for its unusual flight behavior: it will often hold its wings out horizontally and glide. This gives observers a good opportunity to appreciate its striking wing patterning of black and white patches and stripes. Its wings have a background color of black, and the forewings are marked with a diagonal stripe extending from the base and a series of patches forming a broken marginal band. The hindwing has a double band of white patches. From below it is a more brown color and the repeated markings are creamy yellow. Most glider butterflies are found in west Africa or south-east Asia, but this species is unique to Europe.

CATERPILLAR: Feeds on pea plants
WINGSPAN: $1^3/_4$–2 inches
HABITAT: Deciduous woodland, open scrubland, forest steppes
RANGE: From eastern Europe, into Russia toward Japan
STATUS: Locally common

CARDINAL PANDORIANA PANDORA

CATERPILLAR: Black body with orange stripes and spines. Feeds nocturnally on violets
WINGSPAN: 2³/₈–3¹/₈ inches
HABITAT: Woodland edges and clearings
RANGE: Southern Europe into north Africa and Asia
STATUS: Locally common

This European fritillary has an attractive combination of colors on its wings, which distinguishes it from its close relatives. On the upper side the wings are pale orange with black markings, including a band of diamond-shaped spots along the marginal edges of both wings. Spreading out from the base of the wings is a suffusion of pale green scales. On the underside this green is repeated in the background color of the hindwings, which are also marked with delicate white bands, crescents and dots. The forewing tips are also pale green, while the remainder of the wing is a rosy pink with black spots.

PARTHENOS SYLVIA CLIPPER

This relatively large, broad-winged butterfly is a strong, swift flier. It has dark brown to orange-brown colored wings, bearing variable patterns of paler brown stripes, crescents and patches and a number of translucent white patches on the forewing edges and tips. The underside of the wings tends to be similarly patterned, but paler than above, and its body is ringed with dark brown and orange. Rather confusingly, across some areas in its range there are varieties of Clipper with dark blue and green background colors; however, the white patches on the forewings are a clear identifying feature. The Clipper can often be observed basking along stream edges in large numbers.

CATERPILLAR: Olive-green with purple spines. Feeds on adenia
WINGSPAN: 4–4³/₈ inches
HABITAT: Tropical forests, particularly edges and clearings
RANGE: From India and Sri Lanka across south-east Asia to New Guinea
STATUS: Generally common

PEARL CRESCENT

PHYCIODES THAROS

The caterpillar of the Pearl Crescent feeds on asters: in meadows abundant with the flower, swarms of hundreds of these butterflies can be found. From above, the wings are orange with black borders and black markings, including veining, patches and spots. The underwings are a creamy yellow with brown veins. There are two distinct brown patches on the forewing and on the hindwing a pale crescent-shaped spot, hence its common name.

CATERPILLAR: Black body with fine white stripes on back and sides and dark spines. Feeds on aster
WINGSPAN: 1–1³⁄₈ inches
HABITAT: Damp and dry meadows, prairies, woodland edges, roadsides and yards
RANGE: Across North America from Canada to Mexico
STATUS: Common and widespread

COMMA
POLYGONIA C-ALBUM

CATERPILLAR: Black body with orange stripes, a white patch behind the neck and spines. Feeds on nettles and hops

WINGSPAN: 1 ½–2 ⅜ inches

HABITAT: Flowery woodland, meadows, yards, wasteland, and roadsides

RANGE: Western and southern Europe, into Asia and north Africa

STATUS: Widespread and common

This butterfly has two main distinguishing features: its untidily scalloped wing-edges and brown underside enable it to closely resemble a dry leaf when at rest; and it bears a sharp white C mark, or comma, on its hindwing. From above the Comma has a background color of rich orange which is marked with brown patches and spots and rufus edges with pale orange crescents. Its underwing color is mottled brown, patterned to closely resemble a dead leaf. The white comma is in the center of the hindwing. Its forewings are hooked at the top, with deep scallops running down both wing edges and short, rounded tails on the hindwing. It hibernates as a butterfly among dry leaves.

MOTHER-OF-PEARL BUTTERFLY
SALAMIS PARHASSUS

This large, beautiful butterfly has almost translucent wings; they are iridescent pale green shot with purple. In flight its scales catch the light, but at rest it becomes dull: effective camouflage amongst leaves. Its outer edges and hooked forewing tip are black and it has varying black spots on both wings. The hindwings are an irregular, jagged shape, with a short tail that is also black. Above the tail is a bright red, white and black eyespot which deters predators. Mother-of-Pearl Butterflies are unusual for their seasonal differences: during the wet season they are smaller.

CATERPILLAR: Black-brown body with bright red marks on back and spines. Feeds on acanthus

WINGSPAN: 3–4 inches

HABITAT: Dense woodland, rainforests and forest riversides

RANGE: Across Africa south of the Sahara into South Africa

STATUS: Widespread and common

RED ADMIRAL

VANESSA ATALANTA

This is a well-known butterfly across the northern hemisphere, since it is a frequent visitor to yards during the warm summer months. The Red Admiral migrates into the far north of its range in huge numbers; in Europe it is really only native to Mediterranean areas but under the right conditions will make its way to Iceland. Its upper side is a rich blackish brown with bold orange stripes across the forewing and along the hindwing margin. The tip of the forewing is marked with pure white spots. On the underside it is paler; the forewings are brown with patches of orange, white and black, whilst the hindwings have an intricate mottled brown pattern.

CATERPILLAR: Dark gray or green with hairs. Feeds on nettles
WINGSPAN: 2–2³/₈ inches
HABITAT: A wide variety of habitats, wherever flowers and nettles can be found
RANGE: Across the northern hemisphere: from Canada to Central America; Europe into north Africa and India
STATUS: Widespread and common

INDIAN RED ADMIRAL

VANESSA INDICA

This species is very similar to its close relative the Red Admiral; however, it is slightly larger with broader wings and more squared inner hindwings. It is dark brown above with a broad orange band on the forewing which is marked with distinctive black spots. The black forewing tip has smaller white markings. The orange marginal band on the hindwing bears large black spots and there are small blue spots on the inner edge. From below it bears a close resemblance to the Red Admiral.

CATERPILLAR: Black and yellow body with dark spines. Feeds on nettle
WINGSPAN: $2^{3}/_{8}$–$2^{3}/_{4}$ inches
HABITAT: Flowery open land, grassland, meadows, roadsides, gardens
RANGE: From India and Pakistan into Japan and the Philippines
STATUS: Generally common

QUEEN OF SPAIN FRITILLARY
ARGYNNIS LATHONIA

CATERPILLAR: Black body
with white spots, a pair
of white lines along the
back, and brown spines.
Feeds on violets

WINGSPAN: 1½–2 inches

HABITAT: Open lowlands,
fields, meadows and
flowery grassland

RANGE: From north Africa
into Europe and Asia as
far as India

STATUS: Widespread and
common

The Queen of Spain Fritillary is a strong, fast-flying
butterfly which migrates over long distances, reaching
further north in its range during fine weather and even
ascending to over 2,000 feet in search of feeding
territories. From above it has orange wings patterned
with black spots, with the outer wing margins
highlighted by a double row of fine black lines. From
below it has paler forewings with dark spots and
creamy orange hindwings boldly marked with large
silver patches.

SILVER WASHED FRITILLARY
ARGYNNIS PAPHIA

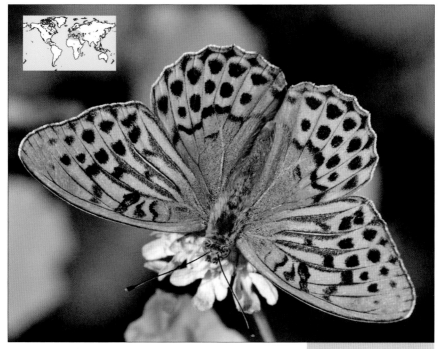

This relatively large fritillary can be identified partly by its size but also by its underside, which is a mixture of pale yellow-green and metallic, silvery white. From above it has typical fritillary markings, a bright orange background color that is patterned with dark blackish brown spots and bars. The spots are organized in two stripes across the margins of both wings, the bars toward the center of the forewing and along the leading edge. Females tend to lack these forewing bars. In both sexes the forewings are angular and long whereas the hindwings are large and rounded.

CATERPILLAR: Dark brown body with a pair of orange back stripes and brown spines. Feeds on violets

WINGSPAN: 2¼–2¾ inches

HABITAT: Woodland, wooded clearings, hedgerows and parkland

RANGE: Across Europe toward north Africa and Asia

STATUS: Widespread and common

SILVER-BORDERED FRITILLARY (SMALL PEARL-BORDERED FRITILLARY)

BOLORIA SELENE

This widespread fritillary is one of the most common types found in North America, where it is known as the Silver-bordered Fritillary. In Europe it is the Small Pearl-bordered Fritillary, and both common names refer to the intricate, metallic patterning on the underside of the hindwing. From above it is deep orange marked with black squares, spots and crescents. The underside forewing is a paler orange with scattered brown markings. The hindwing has a pattern of black veins, spots and orange and white patches. Distinguishing marks include seven white crescent spots on the hindwing margin and a small black eyespot in the center of the hindwing.

CATERPILLAR: Brown body, white markings and pale brown spines. Feeds on violets
WINGSPAN: $1\frac{1}{8}$–$1\frac{1}{2}$ inches
HABITAT: A variety of habitats: woodland, clearings, open lowland and lower mountain slopes—wherever violets grow
RANGE: Across temperate North America, Europe and Asia
STATUS: Generally common

LESSER MARBLED FRITILLARY

BRENTHIS INO

This is a relatively small but otherwise typical fritillary butterfly. It has upper-side wings that are orange marked with a checkered pattern of black spots. The wing-edges are scalloped and bordered with black. Its body and wing bases are also dark. On its underside the wings are more yellow, with black and white edges to both wings. The forewings bear black spots, the hindwings a combination of yellow, brown and buff patches.

CATERPILLAR: Black body with a pair of white stripes and brown back spines. Feeds on raspberry leaves, great burnet, and meadowsweet

WINGSPAN: 1 1/8–1 1/2 inches

HABITAT: Flowery, damp grassland and meadows, marshland

RANGE: Central and northern Europe, excluding the British Isles, into Asia and Japan

STATUS: Locally common

MARSH FRITILLARY EURODRYAS AURINIA

CATERPILLAR: Black body with white spots and spines. Feeds on scabious and plantain
WINGSPAN: 1½–2 inches
HABITAT: Open grassland, marshes, dry moorland
RANGE: Across western Europe toward central Asia
STATUS: Widespread with fluctuating numbers, though generally common

This common fritillary has relatively narrow wings which can aid identification. From above its coloring is an even mixture of orange, cream, and brown in a delicate mosaic patterning. The design of this pattern is not regular but can vary between butterflies from different areas. The wings are edged with a fine white fringe and the dark brown wing border bears small white crescents. It also has small black spots within the orange band that lines the outer margin of the hindwing. Its underside is similarly patterned but with a paler coloring and less black.

MELITAEA DIDYMA SPOTTED FRITILLARY

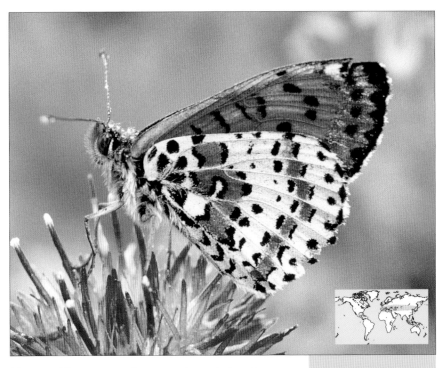

This variable species is always consistent in its wing shape, having broad, rounded wings. Its upper-side background color is usually bright orange, although this can vary from region to region and females are generally paler, particularly on the forewing. Some females are almost gray in color, which can make identification difficult. There is a pattern of black spots and black wing borders and a fine white fringe marked with black. The underside is more regular, with alternating bands of orange and cream marked with black spots.

CATERPILLAR: White with black lines and red back spots plus spines. Feeds on plantains
WINGSPAN: 1 1/8–2 inches
HABITAT: Open, flowery grassland, scrubland, meadows, and roadsides
RANGE: Southern Europe, north Africa and cooler Asia
STATUS: Generally common

GREAT SPANGLED FRITILLARY

SPEYERIA CYBELE

This large fritillary is a common sight across North America, where it can be identified by its combination of dark coloring at the wing bases and bright orange at the outer edges. The broad wings have scalloped edges and these are accentuated by the dark crescent spots on the margins. The forewing also shows a band of dark spots along the edge; smaller spots appear on the hindwing. The orange background color can be paler in some regions. From below the wings show more orange than brown and the hindwing has a number of distinctive silvery spots at the center and the outer edge.

CATERPILLAR: Black with orange spines. Feeds on violets
WINGSPAN: $2^{2}/_{8}$–3 inches
HABITAT: Woodland clearings, meadows, pasture and gardens
RANGE: Across North America from Canada toward New Mexico
STATUS: Common and widespread

REGAL FRITILLARY SPEYERIA IDALIA

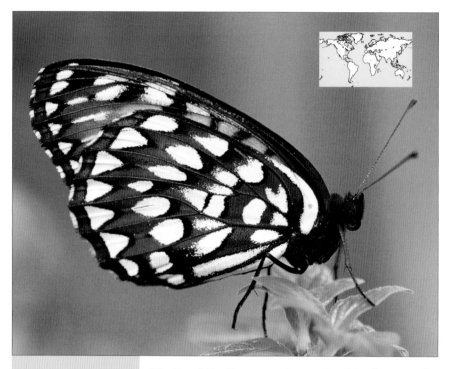

CATERPILLAR: Black and
yellow body with short,
branching spines. Feeds
on bird's-foot and
prairie violets
WINGSPAN: 2¾–3½ inches
HABITAT: Tall-grass prairies
RANGE: Limited to some
states of North America
including Pennsylvania
and Illinois
STATUS: Declining

The Regal Fritillary is a sad example of the detrimental
effect of habitat loss on butterfly populations. This
attractive fritillary is in sharp decline, having
disappeared from many of its former ranges across the
tall-grass prairies of central North America. It is large,
with broad, squared wings. From above the forewings
are a bright orange color with black markings and a
broad black border spotted with white. The hindwings
are black with two rows of marginal white spots. From
below the repeated spotting appears more metallic and
the background color of the wings is similarly dark.

AGLAIS URICAE SMALL TORTOISESHELL

One of Europe's most common and well known butterflies, the Small Tortoiseshell has bright, colorful upperwings that make it easy to recognize. From above the background color is orange-red, marked with square patches of dark brown or black and creamy yellow. These patches form a broad band along the leading edge of the forewing. Along the raggedly scalloped edges of both wings is a broad black border checkered with pale blue spots. On its underside the Small Tortoiseshell is far duller in appearance, with blackish-brown wings with a pale brown border. The forewing bears a pale patch. Late-summer and fall broods will hibernate as butterflies, usually in barns, lofts, and stables.

CATERPILLAR: Yellow-and-black-striped body covered in yellow spines. Groups of caterpillars feed on nettle leaves

WINGSPAN: 2 inches

HABITAT: Open flowery areas: meadows, fields, roadsides, gardens, lower mountain slopes

RANGE: Across Europe into Asia and Japan

STATUS: Common and widespread

MOURNING CLOAK/ CAMBERWELL BEAUTY

NYMPHALIS ANTIOPA

Commonly known as the Mourning Cloak in America and Camberwell Beauty in Europe, this butterfly is widespread but not necessarily easy to observe. As woodland butterflies that feed on tree sap, they only occasionally come down to the ground to feed off flowers. Both males and females are a deep maroon color bordered with light yellow and a band of bright blue spots on the outer edges. From below they are dark gray with black lines and white wing margins speckled with black. The butterfly hibernates in tree hollows over winter, but will often emerge on warm early-spring days.

CATERPILLAR: Black body with white spots and red back markings. Feeds on deciduous trees
WINGSPAN: $2^{3}/_{8}$–$3^{1}/_{8}$ inches
HABITAT: Deciduous woodland, gardens, yards, and parkland; any open lowland with appropriate trees
RANGE: North America, Europe, and cooler regions of Asia
STATUS: Widespread but not common; declining in some areas

LARGE TORTOISESHELL
NYMPHALIS POLYCHLOROS

CATERPILLAR: Black body with white spots and orange spines. Feeds on tree foliage
WINGSPAN: 2–2³/₈ inches
HABITAT: Deciduous woodland, hedgerows, yards; wherever elms and willows can be found
RANGE: From western Europe across to Asia
STATUS: Widespread and generally common, although numbers have suffered through damage to habitat, particularly from diseased elms

The Large Tortoiseshell is bigger and hairier than its small namesake, and is slightly less bright and distinctive. The background color of the upperwings is orange; there are black patches and spots on the forewing and a single patch on the hindwing. The leading edge of the forewing is marked with both black and yellow patches. The ragged wing-edges bear a broad black band marked with yellow, and on the hindwing edge small blue crescents can be observed. The underside is mottled brown with a blue-gray marginal band. The Large Tortoiseshell hibernates as a butterfly, chosing tree hollows, its preferred habitat, and sometimes caves, barns, and sheds. It feeds on tree sap.

GULF FRITILLARY
AGRAULIS VANILLAE

A common butterfly across the southern states of North America, the Gulf Fritillary is a regular visitor to well stocked parks and yards. From above its wings have a background color of bright reddish orange, marked with dark brown streaks and spots. There are three distinguishing black and white eyespots near the leading edge of the forewing; the hindwing has a distinctive dark-ringed border. From below the wings have a more brownish-orange background color, and both bear large, elongated and irregularly shaped silver patches with dark edges. Males and females are similar.

CATERPILLAR: Orange body with rows of black, branching spines. Feeds on passionflowers

WINGSPAN: $2^3/_4$–3 inches

HABITAT: Parks and yards, woodland edges, open scrubland

RANGE: Central America and the West Indies up to southern states of North America

STATUS: Common and widespread

JULIA/FLAMBEAU DRYAS IULIA

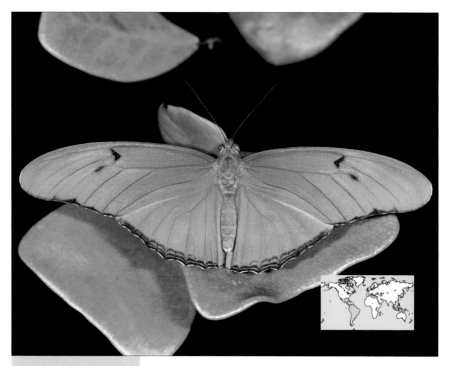

CATERPILLAR: Brown spiny body. Feeds on passionflower
WINGSPAN: 2¾–3½ inches
HABITAT: Subtropical woodland edges, open edges, Florida Everglades
RANGE: From South and Central America up to southern states of the USA
STATUS: Generally common

In some areas the Julia is known as the Flambeau and its long, narrow wings are indeed a flaming orange-red color from above. The bright upperwing is delicately marked with black veins, and whilst males have a dark forewing spot on the leading edge, females have a black band that crosses the forewing. Both sexes are finely edged with black and the scalloped hindwing also bears orange crescent spots. From underneath the Julia is a paler orange-brown with creamy white markings on the hindwing fringe. Typically, this brightly colored butterfly is also poisonous.

HELICONIUS CHARITHONIA ZEBRA

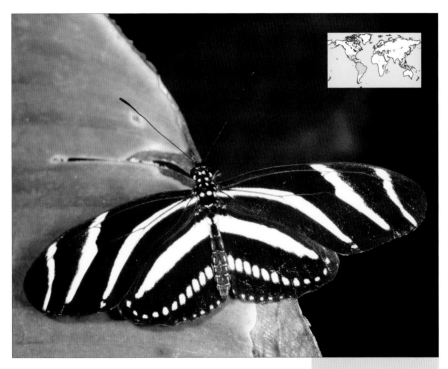

Like many other Heliconius butterflies, the Zebra collects and feeds on the pollen and nectar of forest flowers. It has black wings which are boldly marked with yellow bands, three on the forewing and one solid band across the center of the hindwing, plus a broken band along the hindwing margin. Its underside is similar but with the addition of red spots at the wing bases. In order to ensure a virgin mate, males prefer to mate with females as they are drying after emerging from their pupa.

CATERPILLAR: White body with black spines and spots. Feeds on passionflower

WINGSPAN: $2^{3}/_{4}$–$3^{1}/_{8}$ inches

HABITAT: Dense tropical woodland edges and clearings

RANGE: Southern states of the USA to Central and South America and the West Indies

STATUS: Generally common, although threatened by loss of habitat

HELICONIUS MIMIC

EUEIDES ISABELLA

An attractive mimic butterfly, the Heliconius Mimic or Isabella's Heliconian has broad, narrow, rounded forewings and smaller, rounded hindwings. Its coloration is similar to that of a number of other Heliconius species, poisonous models for a number of mimics. The Isabella has similar markings on both sides of its wings, although it is duller below. The forewings have a background color of brown with orange stripes on the inner, basal edge and yellow patches toward the outer tips. The underwings are broadly striped with orange and brown and the brown marginal edge is marked with small white spots.

CATERPILLAR: Black body with white bands across the back. Feeds on passionflower
WINGSPAN: 2–2¾ inches
HABITAT: Sub-tropical forests, clearings, and edges
RANGE: South and Central America, into southern states of the USA
STATUS: Generally common

THE POSTMAN

HELICONIUS MELPOMENE

This slow-flying butterfly avoids bright sunlight, keeping to the shadier parts of the forest edges which it inhabits. Like other Heliconia it has long, narrow wings, but its coloration is very variable since different subspecies will mimic the subspecies of *Heliconius erato*—the Small Postman. In general it will have a background color of black with a variety of red and yellow markings on both wings. From below, the markings are repeated, but the colors are more muted.

CATERPILLAR: White body with black spots, orange head and spines. Feeds on passionflower
WINGSPAN: $2^{3}/_{8}$–$3^{1}/_{8}$ inches
HABITAT: Subtropical forest edges
RANGE: Central and South America and the West Indies
STATUS: Generally common

SWEET OIL MECHANITIS POLYMNIA

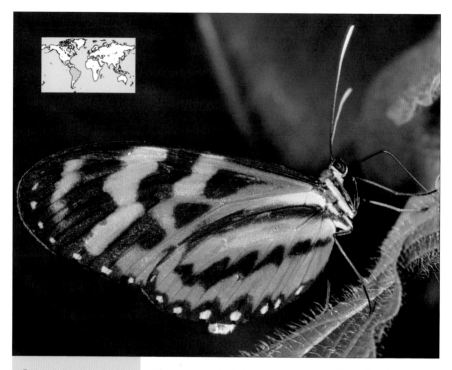

CATERPILLAR: Pale green back and yellow sides with yellow side spines. Feeds on solanum leaves, particularly deadly nightshade
WINGSPAN: $2^3/_8$–3 inches
HABITAT: A variety of habitats, including forest edges, fields, roadsides and urban areas
RANGE: From Mexico into South America
STATUS: Generally common

This is a particularly common butterfly in South America and is regularly seen flying through built-up areas and city streets. Its ability to adapt to disrupted habitats has earned it the alternative common name Disturbed Tigerwing. A poisonous species, it is the model for a large number of mimics. It has a long, narrow forewing which is orange at the base then yellow leading to a black tip. The colored wing is marked with black patches. The hindwings are orange with a broad central black band and a black margin. On the underside both wing margins are spotted with blue.

DANAUS CHRYSIPPUS PLAIN TIGER

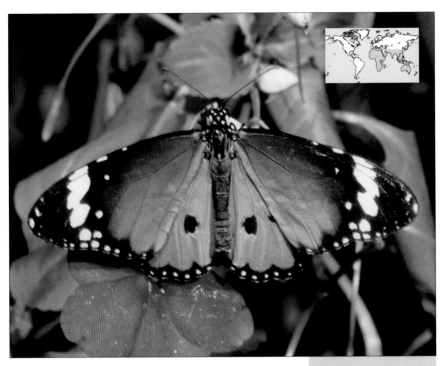

This butterfly is also known as the African Monarch, due to its familial resemblance to its close relative *Danaus plexippus*. It is a strong flier, with a slow, bouncing flight style, and migrates long distances. It has broad, pointed forewings which are orange in color with black tips bearing white spots. The hindwings are creamy white with orange and black edges and a series of dark spots in the center of the wing; the number of these varies between different individuals. The underside is similar but paler. As a successful poisonous butterfly, the Plain Tiger is the model for a number of mimics.

CATERPILLAR: Orange-, black- and white-banded body. Feeds on milkweed

WINGSPAN: $2\frac{3}{4}$–$3\frac{1}{8}$ inches

HABITAT: A variety: open fields, gardens, forests edges

RANGE: Across Africa, Asia, Australia, Japan and Malaysia

STATUS: Widespread and common

QUEEN

DANAUS GILIPPUS

In appearance the Queen butterfly is similar to its close relative the Monarch; however it is smaller in size and slightly darker in appearance, with far less patterning on the upper side. From above the background color of the wings is a deep orange-brown with darker brown wing margins. There are white spots on the tip of the forewing and scattered along the margins. Males also show scent scales on the center hindwing as a small pale-gray mark. The underside is a slightly paler orange-brown with distinctive black veins edged with white. The white spots on the black wing margins are bold, as are the white spots marking the black body and abdomen.

CATERPILLAR: Gray body with black rings spotted with orange. Feeds on milkweed
WINGSPAN: 2¾–3 inches
HABITAT: Open areas, grassland, scrub, deserts, and prairies
RANGE: Southern states of the USA into Central and South America
STATUS: Common

MONARCH

DANAUS PLEXIPPUS

This well known migrant is a striking orange color with distinctive black veining, a warning to predators that it is poisonous. Both wings bear black marginal bands marked with bright white spots, a pattern that is repeated on its body and abdomen. The pointed forewings have a black tip which has three distinctive orange patches. The underside is similar but paler, and males have a small black scent patch on their hindwings. A very strong flier, swarms of Monarchs travel in huge numbers heading south from Canada to Mexico during fall. When the wind blows in the right direction many are swept off course toward Europe and Australasia.

CATERPILLAR: Black, yellow and cream bands with black tentacles behind the head. Feeds on milkweed
WINGSPAN: 2¾–4 inches
HABITAT: Open land, fields, roadsides, prairies and gardens
RANGE: Native to the Americas, vagrant to Australasia, the Canary Islands, and Europe
STATUS: Common in the Americas, scarcer in migrant countries

HESPERIIDAE
SKIPPERS

ARCTIC SKIPPER
CARTEROCEPHALUS PALAEMON

CATERPILLAR: Pale creamy brown with pink stripes. Feeds on grasses
WINGSPAN: $^3/_4$–1$^1/_8$ inches
HABITAT: Grassland, woodland edges, and clearings
RANGE: Cold and temperate North America, Europe, and Asia
STATUS: Widespread and common

The distinctive patterning on this widespread skipper makes it relatively easy to identify, particularly since it likes to rest with its wings open. It has upperwings that are predominantly dark brown with orange markings arranged in a checkerboard pattern. On the underside the color is much paler with the marking repeated in a buff color. Males are highly territorial and can be observed keeping watch over their area from tree branches or tall grasses. It has a preference for colder climates, hence its common name (although in Europe is called the Checkered Skipper). Like many skippers, the adult Arctic Skipper lay eggs singly on the leaves of grasses. The young caterpillar creates a tent by pulling the edges of the leaves together and binding them with silk threads.

SILVER-SPOTTED SKIPPER
EPARGYREUS CLARUS

Skippers are called so because of their habit of flying from plant to plant in short "skips." There are over 3,000 different species. The Silver-spotted Skipper is one of the most conspicuous, being is a relatively large skipper, with elongated hindwings and small, blunt tails. On its upperside the Silver-spotted Skipper has a background color of dark brown with orange patches on the forewing. This patch is repeated on the underside of the butterfly, but the coloring is much paler and more translucent. The butterfly earns it common name from the distinctive silver patch that marks the center of the underside hindwing. It has a distinctively wide head, and antennae with a curved tip.

CATERPILLAR: Light green with darker patches and a red head
WINGSPAN: 1½–2⅜ inches
HABITAT: Woodland edges, brush, and fields
RANGE: Found across North America
STATUS: Widespread and common

LARGE SKIPPER

OCHLODES VENATAS

The Large Skipper has a background color of olive-brown on its wings, which in males is suffused with orange, making them much brighter. Males can also be distinguished by their sex brand, the black line on the forewing which is formed from scent scales. Its wings are a rich ruddy brown above and much paler yellow-brown below, and on the upper side the veins are displayed in a darker blackish brown. Females tend to be duller, with a darker background brown which bears dull yellow spots on both upper-side wings. When at rest it holds its wings open at a slight angle, enabling identification with a view of both sides.

CATERPILLAR: Green body. Feeds on grasses
WINGSPAN: 1 $\frac{1}{8}$ inches
HABITAT: Open grassland, woodland edges and
    clearings, flowery meadows, and hedgerows
RANGE: Across Europe into Asia as far as Japan
STATUS: Generally common

DINGY SKIPPER _ERYNNIS TAGES_

CATERPILLAR: Pale green with a black line along back, and black head. Feeds on members of the pea family, particularly crown vetch

WINGSPAN: 1 inch

HABITAT: Flowery grassland, meadows, and lower mountain slopes

RANGE: Western and northern Europe into northern Asia and China

STATUS: Common, though numbers are in decline

Often found in meadows and grassland, this small brown butterfly could easily be mistaken for a moth (such as the Mother Shipton moth) with its stout abdomen and buzzing flight. It also resembles the Grizzled Skipper which can be similar in color. Its dark mottled upperwings provide excellent camouflage; the forewings are patterned with dark brown on a grayish-brown background, while the hindwings are brown with small white spots along the marginal edge. From below, the Dingy Skipper is a paler brown with the white marginal spots repeated. It has a preference for cooler climates.

PYRGUS MALVAE GRIZZLED SKIPPER

The Grizzled Skipper is a widespread but unfortunately declining example of the genus *Pyrgus*, skippers with white spot markings. It has the characteristic skipper shape, with the length of the body and wings being roughly equal (in other butterflies the wings tend to be longer). On its upper side the background color is brown and this bears small, squarish, white spots in a checkered pattern. The wing-edges are uniformly checkered in brown and white. It is paler on the underside and the white markings are larger, particularly on the hindwing, which bears a large central white patch. Its body is darker above and paler below, mirroring the colors of the wings.

CATERPILLAR: Green with a large black head. Feeds on potentilla and wild strawberry

WINGSPAN: $^{3}/_{4}$–1 inch

HABITAT: Woodland edges and clearings, heaths, grassy meadows

RANGE: Across Europe into Asia toward Mongolia

STATUS: Locally common, but in decline

LULWORTH SKIPPER

THYMELICUS ACTION

This is a fast-flying and active little butterfly which can be found on a range of grasslands. The background color of its wings is an olive brown, and on females the forewing shows delicate patches of yellow on the upper side. Males are marked with a fine black line across the forewing and their wing color is more yellowy than the females'. When basking, the Lulworth Skipper raises its forewings slightly, while keeping the hindwings in a horizontal position. This typical skipper attitude is thought to aid the absorption of the sun's energy.

CATERPILLAR: Pale green, with darker green back. Feeds on grasses
WINGSPAN: 1 inch
HABITAT: Open grassland and meadows
RANGE: Western and southern Europe into Asia
STATUS: Generally common

EUROPEAN SKIPPER THYMELICUS LINEOLA

CATERPILLAR: Pale green with yellow stripes. Feeds on grasses
WINGSPAN: 1 inch
HABITAT: Flowery fields, meadows, roadside verges
RANGE: North Africa, Europe and Asia, North America
STATUS: Generally common

Almost identical to its close relative the Small Skipper (*Thymelicus sylvestris*), the European Skipper can be distinguished only by the darker color of its antennae. Unlike many other skippers, it overwinters as an egg rather than a caterpillar. Its wings are an attractive rusty orange color on both sides, the only significant markings are the slightly darker wing-edges and the paler fringe. It is fairly widespread: in areas inhabited by European Skippers, they can appear in large numbers. In the United States and Canada this is an introduced butterfly. European Skipper is known as the Essex Skipper in Europe.

URBANUS PROTEUS LONG-TAILED SKIPPER

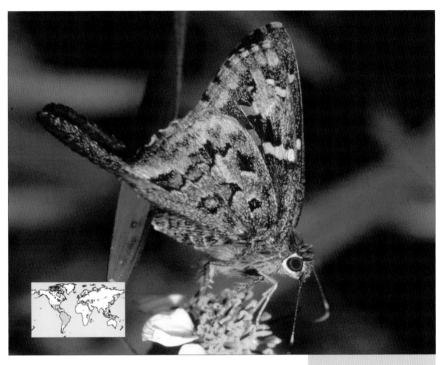

In most respects this is a typical skipper butterfly. However, it has two remarkable distinguishing features: proportionally long tail streamers and an iridescent-green coloring on the upper side of the wings. From above, the wings are rich brown in color with a series of white patches on the tips of the forewings. The hindwings and tails are a similar brown without any markings. The green scaling extends from the body and base of the wings and reaches on to the tails. From below, both wings show brown, black and white patterning, while the tails are solid brown. In the southern states of the United States this attractive butterfly can become a pest in bean crops, where it is known as the "bean leaf roller."

CATERPILLAR: Olive body with brown stripes, yellow and black spots. Feeds on phaseolus

WINGSPAN: $1\frac{1}{2}$–$2\frac{1}{4}$ inches

HABITAT: Open fields, scrubland, wasteland, and agricultural land

RANGE: From South America up toward southern states of the USA

STATUS: Generally common

SATYRIIDAE
SATYRS AND BROWNS

RINGLET APHANTOPUS HYPERANTUS

CATERPILLAR: Pale olive green, with fine yellow and black stripes. Feeds on grasses
WINGSPAN: 1½–2 inches
HABITAT: Low-level open grassland, meadows, roadside verges, hedgerows, and woodland edges
RANGE: Across Europe into Asia
STATUS: Widespread and common

The Ringlet is a common European and Asian butterfly, and a typical example of a Satyr; it is small and brown and bears a prominent band of small eyespots. On its upper side the Ringlet is dark brown; in males this can be almost black. Each wing bears a pair of small dark eyespots, which are not always apparent. The underside is a much paler brown and the eyespots are highly visible, black ringed with yellow with a white highlight. There are often five eyespots on the hindwing and three on the fore; however the number and size of these distinctive markings does vary. It is thought that these eyespots confuse predators as to the position of the butterfly's body.

COENONYMPHA ARCANIA PEARLY HEATH

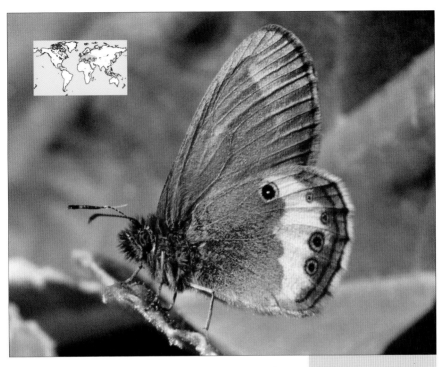

This small, European grassland butterfly rarely reveals its upperwings when resting, but when flying it is possible to see a flash of its orange wings. Its upper side is mainly brown, with orange forewings edged with dark brown. On the underside, the orange-brown forewing bears a small black eyespot with white highlight. The hindwing is gray-brown with a buff-colored steak and an orange marginal band. There are several eyespots lined along the marginal edge; these are black ringed with orange with a white highlight. An additional eyespot can be observed on the inner edge of the hindwing.

CATERPILLAR: Green with white side stripe. Feeds on grasses
WINGSPAN: $1^3/_8$ inches
HABITAT: Grassy slopes, mountain foothills, and open woodland
RANGE: Across western Europe into western Asia
STATUS: Generally common

SMALL HEATH COENONYMPHA PAMPHILUS

CATERPILLAR: Pale green body with yellow stripes. Feeds on grasses
WINGSAPN: 1³/₈ inches
HABITAT: Open grassland, meadows, and roadside verges
RANGE: Across northern Europe, including Britain and Scandinavia
STATUS: Locally common, threatened by loss of habitat

On its upper side the Small Heath has solid orange-brown forewings, and similarly colored hindwings with a pale patch at the inner edge and gray borders. From below it is more gray, with gray hindwings that are distinguished by a pale wavy band across the center of the wing. The forewing is orange-brown with gray margins and a pale-ringed black eyespot with white highlight. Since the Small Heath tends to rest with its wings closed, its underside is that which is most often observed. The male and female look very similar, the main distinction being that the female is slightly larger.

COENONYMPHA TULLIA (AMERICAN) RINGLET

In Europe this butterfly is commonly known as the Large Heath, in North America as the Ringlet, and in appearance it is not too dissimilar from the European Ringlet. This neat little grassland butterfly has a variable background coloring, from creamy yellow to brown; however, its distinguishing feature is the eyespots, which are more bold on the underside of the wings. There is always a small round black eyespot on the tip of the forewing; this is both ringed and highlighted with white on the underside. On the hindwing there is a row of similar eyespots, the number of which can vary. The Large Heath has a characteristic flight pattern, keeping close the ground on windy days.

CATERPILLAR: Green body, dark green back, and white side stripes. Feeds on sedge and cottongrass

WINGSPAN: 1 inches

HABITAT: Grasses, hillsides, meadows, and lower mountain slopes

RANGE: Central and northern Europe into Asia, across the United States into Canada

STATUS: Widespread and common

LITTLE WOOD SATYR

EUPTYCHIA CYMELA

The eyespots on this Satyr are its most distinguishing feature. It has rich-brown wings edged with a pair of fine dark lines. The pair of eyespots on each wing are black and ringed with orange, and each bears a pair of silvery-blue highlights. On its underside the Little Wood Satyr is a paler brown color and the prominent eyespots are repeated. The outer wing margins are marked with a series of fine stripes and the eyespots are connected by a series of small metallic spots. These butterflies can occasionally be observed feeding from bird droppings.

CATERPILLAR: Brown body with tiny white spots. Feeds on grasses
WINGSPAN: $1^{3}/_{4}$–2 inches
HABITAT: Brushland, wooded clearings, and woodland edges
RANGE: Across eastern half of North America, from Canada to Mexico
STATUS: Generally common

GRAYLING HIPPARCHIA SEMELE

CATERPILLAR: Brown body with black stripes. Feeds on grasses
WINGSPAN: 2 inches
HABITAT: Dry rocky grassland and cliffs, meadows and lower mountain slopes
RANGE: Across Europe into Asia
STATUS: Generally common

This small butterfly is an expert at camouflage; it likes to bask on tree trunks and bare rock, and not only is its wing pattern designed to merge in with such a background, it also holds its wings at a slight angle to avoid casting any shadow. On its upper side it has pale, dull-brown wings with buff and orange patches and brown eyespots. The underwings, which are more likely to be observed, are mottled gray and brown on the hindwing. The brighter forewing is often tucked behind the resting hindwing, whereby its buff and orange patch and two black eyespots are less noticeable to predators.

MANIOLA TITHONIUS GATEKEEPER

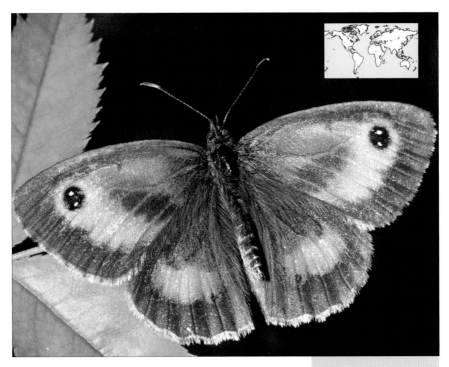

This particularly common member of the brown family is in abundance during midsummer, particularly when brambles are in flower. It is a small butterfly, with bright orange upperwings that are broadly bordered with brown across both wing margins. The forewing also bears a brown central patch and a black eyespot marked with a pair of white highlights. Males also bear a dark sex patch on the forewing. On the underside both wings are much paler, a buff yellow on the forewing and marbled lighter browns on the hindwing. The forewing eyespot is repeated below.

CATERPILLAR: Green body with darker green side stripes. Feeds on grasses
WINGSPAN: 1½ inches
HABITAT: Open grassy land, meadows, hedgerows, and woodland edges
RANGE: Across western and southern Europe toward Turkey
STATUS: Generally common

MEADOW BROWN

MANIOLA JURTINA

This common grassland butterfly is a strong, fast flier and the males are highly territorial, patrolling their area keeping watch for other males. Identification is easier when the underside is observed, since the upper side of the Meadow Brown is particularly variable, both between the sexes and across the range. In general from above it is a rich brown color with an orange patch near the tip of the forewing which bears the large dark eyespot. Females are more sharply colored, often showing far more orange than the males, many of which can show no orange at all. From below the wings are much paler: the forewing is orange and buff brown with the dark eyespot, the hindwing brown with a broad buff band which bears small dark spots.

CATERPILLAR: Green body with yellow side stripe and yellow hairs. Feeds on grasses
WINGSPAN: 2 inches
HABITAT: Grassland, meadows, roadsides, woodland edges, and clearings
RANGE: Across Europe into central Asia
STATUS: Widespread and common

MARBLED WHITE

MELANGARIA GALATHEA

This is an attractive black-and-white-patterned butterfly with a very apt common name. On the upper side of its wings it is distinctively grounded with dark blackish brown which bears a marbled pattern of white patches. There is a large basal patch on both wings and also white crescents on the brown margins. On the underside, more white shows, with black veins and gray patches as well as a black line edging the outer wing margins. There is also a gray band marked with eyespots on the hindwing. Males and females are similar, although females have a yellowish hindwing on the underside.

CATERPILLAR: Pale green with dark line along the back. Feeds on grasses
WINGSPAN: 2 inches
HABITAT: Low-lying, flowery grassland, meadows, and roadside verges
RANGE: Western and central Europe into north Africa and Asia
STATUS: Widespread and commonly found in colonies

DRYAD BUTTERFLY MINIOS DRYAS

CATERPILLAR: Creamy white speckled with dark and two brown stripes extending from the forked tail. Feeds on grasses
WINGSPAN: 2–2¾ inches
HABITAT: Dry, open grassland, low slopes, and open woodland
RANGE: Southern Europe into Asia and Japan
STATUS: Locally common

Male and female Dryad Butterflies are dimorphic, or dissimilar; however both are relatively easy to identify, for different reasons. The male is smaller and has upperwings which are almost solid black; the forewing, however, bears a pair of blue eyespots that are almost impossible to see. From underneath it is mottled gray and brown and the forewing bears a single dark eyespot. The female is much paler, with upperwings that are rich brown, and the two blue eyespots are a prominent feature, as is the single blue eyespot on the hindwing. The underside is similar to that of the male. Both sexes have scalloped hindwings; this feature is much more pronounced in the female.

PARARGE AEGERIA SPECKLED WOOD

The speckled brown patterning on this woodland
butterfly gives it effective camouflage in the dappled
light of its woodland habitat. On its upper side it has a
background color of rich brown which is marked on the
forewings with creamy yellow patches and on the
hindwing with a row of bold eyespots—black ringed
with cream and highlighted with white. The markings on
the hindwings can appear orange in some areas,
particularly in the south of its range. On its underside
the hindwing eyespots are less clear to see, lacking the
black; however the forewing bears a more prominent
black spot at the tip. The underside has a more marbled
brown appearance. Like several other butterflies (notably
the skippers) the Speckled Brown shows a high degree of
territorial behavior.

CATERPILLAR: Pale green
with dark green back
and fine side stripes.
Feeds on couch grass
WINGSPAN: 1³/₄ inches
HABITAT: Mature,
deciduous woodland
RANGE: Across Europe
into Asia
STATUS: Common in its
habitat

WALL BROWN

PARARGE MEGERA

This striking orange Satyr can often be observed sunbathing with its wings spread open. It has upperwings grounded in rich orange and patterned with dark veins, bands and patches. Its gently scalloped and rounded wings are edged with dark brown and the pale fringe is checkered with brown. There is a row of black eyespots hightlighted with white on the hindwing and one prominent and similar eyespot on the forewing. On its underside the patterning is repeated on to a paler background of buff, gray and brown. The hindwing is almost marbled in these colors, a design that provides effective camouflage.

CATERPILLAR: Green with a white side stripe. Feeds on grasses
WINGSPAN: 1³⁄₄ inches
HABITAT: Dry heaths, hillsides, and cliffs
RANGE: Across Europe into Asia
STATUS: Although widespread, the Wall Brown is in general decline

MOTHS

GARDEN TIGER MOTH

ARCTIA CAJA

This beautiful moth has strikingly different markings on its forewings and hindwings. The forewings have a creamy white background which is marked with either dark brown or black patches, a design that provides effective camouflage in the still moth. The hindwings are a contrasting flame-orange color with black-ringed gray spots. The body is also orange, marked with black bands. A startled Garden Tiger will flash its bright hindwings which alarms any potential predator. Like most Arctid moths, its caterpillar is covered in poisonous spines and is commonly referred to as a "woolly bear."

CATERPILLAR: Black body covered in long black hairs with red hairs at the base. Feeds on a variety of low shrubs
WINGSPAN: 2–2¾ inches
HABITAT: Parks and yards and other cultivated land, roadsides, wasteland
RANGE: Mainly Europe into cooler Asia across to Japan. Also found in North America
STATUS: Widespread but declining, particularly in North America

GIANT LEOPARD MOTH
HYPERCOMPE SCRIBONIA

CATERPILLAR: Black hairy body, with usually invisible scarlet rings along segments
WINGSPAN: $2^{3}/_{8}$–$3^{1}/_{2}$ inches
HABITAT: Agricultural land, orchards, woodland edges, parks, and yards
RANGE: From southeastern Canada down through eastern United states toward Mexico
STATUS: Generally common

A relatively large Arctid moth, the Giant Leopard Moth has strikingly patterned forewings which aid identification. The background color is pure white covered with dark brown, ring-like markings and solid spots; this is continued on the moth's thorax and the back of its head. The hindwings lack these ring markings, instead they are solid white with dark brown spots along the outer edges. Males and females are similar, although the male has a dark yellowish-brown margin along the inner edge of the hindwing which the larger female lacks. The moth's abdomen is blue-black marked with dark yellow spots and its black legs have distinctive white bands.

WHITE ERMINE
SPILOSOMA LUBRICIPEDA

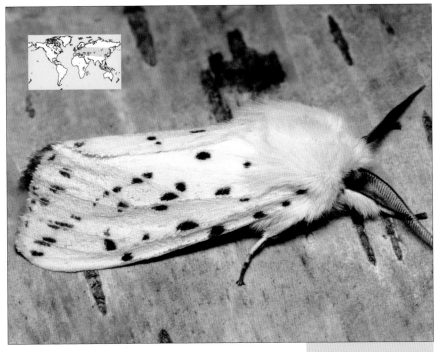

This relatively small Arctid moth has forewings that closely resemble the fur of its mammalian namesake, being pure white with black dots. Its hindwings are predominantly white; the only significant marking is a black spot on the inner edge of the wing. Its abdomen is a bright orange color with lines of black spots, a warning to potential predators of its inedible status. The head and thorax are covered in white fur. In some areas color variations can be found: the white can be more creamy yellow, or alternatively more or fewer black spots can be seen.

CATERPILLAR: Black hairy body with red-colored line along back. Fast moving and feeds on most plants
WINGSPAN: 1$\frac{1}{8}$–2 inches
HABITAT: Found in a wide variety of habitats
RANGE: Across Europe and Asia toward Japan
STATUS: Widespread and common

SILKMOTH

BOMBYX MORI

Possibly the most famous moth of all, the Silkmoth is a member of the Bombycid family, most of which are native to east Asia and all of which spin strong silken cocoons. The *Bombyx mori* is the moth most usually associated with the production of silk for human use, and it has been bred in captivity for over 4,000 years so that it now no longer exists in the wild. Its wings are a creamy white or pale brown color with visible veins and a slight hook at the forewing tip. Its stocky, furred body matches the wing coloring and the head lacks mouthparts, leaving it unable to feed as an adult. It is the caterpillars that provide the silk, and these are commercially raised in huge numbers; they do not survive the silk-extraction process.

CATERPILLAR: Pale, white body with pinkish eyespots along the back. Fed on Mulberry leaves
WINGSPAN: $1\frac{1}{2}$–$2\frac{3}{8}$ inches
HABITAT: Bred in captivity
RANGE: Originated in China
STATUS: Wild colonies are extinct; huge numbers in captivity worldwide

OWL MOTH

BRAHMAEA WALLICHII

This large moth is a striking example of the small Brahmaeid family—large, brown, highly patterned moths. The Owl Moth earns its name from the large owl's-eye-like eyespots at the base of the forewing. Both wings have a background color of rich brown which is intricately patterned with regular bars and waves of darker brown. The solid-brown forewing tips bear rows of white crescents and both wings are bordered with pale brown then decorated with brown and white crescents. The eyespots bear three or more small dark dots. Its stocky body is dark brown banded and striped with pale brown.

CATERPILLAR: White and yellow body with black spots. Feeds on ash, privet, and liliac.
WINGSPAN: 3–6¼ inches
HABITAT: Open woodland, both deciduous and sub tropical
RANGE: East Asia, from India to China and Japan
STATUS: Generally locally common

LARGE EMERALD GEOMETRA PAPILIONARIA

CATERPILLAR: Pale green looper. Feeds on birch and alder trees
WINGSPAN: 2–2⅝ inches
HABITAT: Open woodland and forest edges, heathland.
RANGE: Across Europe, into Asia toward Japan
STATUS:Widespread and common

This large, robust Geometrid moth has, as its name suggests, bright green wing coloring. Freshly emerged examples are the most vivid, the solid green contrasting clearly with a a pair of delicate white scalloped lines which run across both wings. Older examples and displayed specimens tend to be faded, becoming a paler gray-green color. The wings are broad and the hindwings in particular are gently scalloped at the rounded outer edges. Although males and females are similar, males can be identified by their more feathered antennae.

LYCIA HIRTARIA BRINDLED BEAUTY

The Brindled Beauty is a brown and white European example of a Geometrid moth. It is particularly effective at camouflage and as a consequence its coloring will vary depending upon its chosen habitat; species in more industrialized areas will often be darker. It rests upon tree trunks, and therefore both wings are a mottled brown and white to resemble bark. Its stocky body is furred, as are its wings – both sexes are able to fly. The male has broadly feathered antennae and tends to be a darker color. Typically, its caterpillar is a looper.

CATERPILLAR: Dark brown or olive green with pale spots. Feeds on tree foliage

WINGSPAN: 1½–2 inches

HABITAT: Open woodland, orchards, parks, and yards

RANGE: Across western and northern Europe

STATUS: Very common; caterpillar can be considered a pest

SWALLOWTAILED MOTH

OURAPTERYX SAMUBUCARIA

A relatively large Geometrid, the Swallow-tailed moth has a particularly striking appearance and if discovered by day is often mistaken for a butterfly. It is however, a nocturnal moth and is more usually observed resting on lighted windows. Its wings are broad and the forewings are pointed whilst the hindwings bear short pointed, tails similar to those found on Swallowtail butterflies. Both wings are a pale creamy yellow color and the forewing is marked by a pair of brown vertical lines, with only one similar line on the hindwing. The hindwing tails are emphasized by small brown spots at the base.

CATERPILLAR: Slender, brown body with pale side stripes. Feeds on hawthorn, ivy, and privet
WINGSPAN: 2–2¹/₂ inches
HABITAT: Hedgerows, woodland, parks, and yards
RANGE: Across Europe into temperate Asia
STATUS: Relatively common

EASTERN TENT CATERPILLAR MOTH
MALACOSOMA AMERICANUM

CATERPILLAR: Dark gray, hairy body with blue and red patches. Feeds on a variety of tree and shrub leaves

WINGSPAN: 1½–2 inches

HABITAT: Deciduous woodland, orchards, parks and yards

RANGE: Across the eastern half of North America, from southern Canada into the United States

STATUS: Common and widespread

This moth is a member of the Lasiocampidae family, commonly referred to as lappet moths, which have no tongues, connected wings, and generally hairy bodies. The Eastern Tent Caterpillar Moth shows all these characteristics: its stout body is covered in brown hair. Its wings are solid brown in color, varying from a peachy light color to much darker; however, all varieties have a pair of distinctive white stripes across the forewing and these are often infilled with white, creating a broad, pale band. The caterpillars live communally in white, silken tents, hence its common name.

GASTROPACHA QUERCIFOLIA LAPPET MOTH

Like most Lasiocampid moths, the Lappet Moth has a stocky body which is also furry. It is a rich red-brown color throughout and the wings can appear to have a purplish sheen. Both the forewings and the hindwings are marked with delicate brown lines which are slightly scalloped. The wings themselves are broadly scalloped, the forewings larger than the rounded hindwings. When the moth is at rest, it holds its wings more upright than most other moths, providing it with effective camouflage when amongst dead leaves. Males and females are similar although female is larger.

CATERPILLAR: Lumpy gray body with brown hairs. Feeds on hawthorn and blackthorn

WINGSPAN: 1½–3 inches

HABITAT: Woodland, forest clearings and hedgerows, parks, and yards

RANGE: From Europe into Asia, China, and Japan

STATUS: Generally common

OAK EGGAR

LASIOCAMPA QUERCUS

The male Oak Eggar can be easily identified by its contrasting brown coloring on both wings. Toward the base it is a rich chocolate brown which is then edged with a broad marginal band of pale yellow-brown. Although the depth of the brown coloring can vary across its range, the forewing always bears a single black-ringed white spot. This marking also appears on the significantly larger female, whose wing coloring is much paler. Males fly during the day, whereas the female is nocturnal. The male can also be identified by his feathered antennae which enable him to find the scent of the female.

CATERPILLAR: Dark brown with black rings and orange hairs. Feeds on oak, brambles, hawthorn, and heather
WINGSPAN: 2–3$\frac{1}{2}$ inches
HABITAT: Woodland, moorland, hedgerows
RANGE: Across Europe into north Africa
STATUS: Generally common

GYPSY MOTH

LYMANTRIA DISPAR

The Gypsy Moth is a daytime flier. However, observers will only ever see a male in flight: the female, although winged, does not fly at all, a typical characteristic of the Lymantriidae family. Males and females are very different: the male is smaller with mottled brown, orange and yellow forewings, and solid yellow-brown hindwings which are bordered with white and dark brown checkering; the female has creamy white wings with simple dark markings on the forewings, including a characteristic V shape near the leading edges. The borders of both wings are checkered white and black. Her body is very large and when carrying a huge egg sac it doubles in size.

CATERPILLAR: Gray body with red and blue tufted spots along the back. Feeds voraciously on on oaks and other trees and shrubs
WINGSPAN: 1½–2¼ inches
HABITAT: Mature deciduous woodland, a variety of wooded areas, meadows, orchards, parks, and yards
RANGE: Widespread; native to Europe and Asia, introduced to North America in the nineteenth century.
STATUS: Very common. Considered a serious pest in North America

BLACK WITCH ASCALAPHA ODORATA

CATERPILLAR: Dark brown body. Feeds on cassia
WINGSPAN: $4^1/_4$–6 inches
HABITAT: A variety of habitats, including woodland, meadows, parks, and yards
RANGE: Across North America, occasionally Canada, down toward Central America
STATUS: Common and widespread

Although a seemingly dull brown moth, the Black Witch has a number of distinguishing features. Its long, pointed forewing has a kidney-shaped eyespot toward the center of the leading edge and this is colored a metallic blue, a sharp contrast to the deep-brown-mottled wing. On the squared hindwing there is a large eyespot which is sharply toothed toward the outer margin and this too is suffused with metallic-blue scales. The scalloped hindwing edges are bordered with darker brown bands. Females have a slightly pinkish band that runs across both wings. The Black Witch is a strong flier, like most Noctuid moths, and will migrate long distances.

THYSANIA AGRIPPINA GIANT AGRIPPA

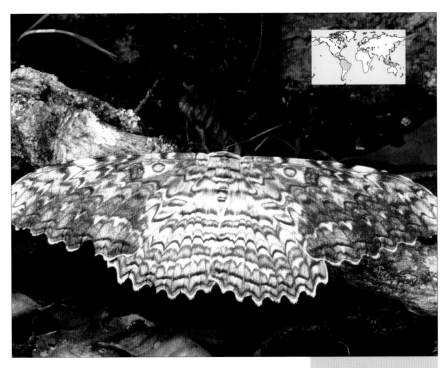

This striking, broad-winged moth has the widest wingspan of any moth in the world—indeed of any butterfly. Its wings are a gray-white color marked with delicate and intricate dark brown lines and chevrons. Both wings are gently scalloped and the margins are lined with deeper, brown scallops, the pattern of which is repeated up through to the base of the wings. Close to the leading edge of the forewing is a small, distinctive brown eyespot, which appears rather square. Its pale body is banded with dark brown.

CATERPILLAR: Feeds on leguminous plants
WINGSPAN: 9–12 inches
HABITAT: Tropical and subtropical forest and woodland
RANGE: Across Central and South America to southern Brazil
STATUS: Generally common

PUSS MOTH CERURA VINULA

CATERPILLAR: Bright green body with dark purple saddle in center of back. Feeds on willow, sallow, and poplar
WINGSPAN: $2^3/_8$–$3^1/_8$ inches
HABITAT: Open woodland, parks and yards, often close to water
RANGE: Across Europe into Asia
STATUS: Widespread and common

The Puss is a member of the Notodontidae or "Prominent" family, whose moths have long forewings, which are often tufted with fine scales. The Puss Moth is perhaps less remarkable than its caterpillar. Its forewings are patterned with a zig-zag marbling of buff-brown and gray, whereas its gray-brown hindwings lack markings other than darker veins. Its long, broad body is furred with a striped abdomen and at the base of the forewings are white scales. Its striking caterpillar effectively deals with predators by whipping out long pink filaments from its forked tails and by squirting formic acid from its throat. When threatened it raises its head, showing a pink "face" with false "eyes."

PTEROPHORUS PENTADACTYLA WHITE PLUME MOTH

This pure-white moth is a member of the Pterophoridae family, commonly known as plume moths since their wings have the appearance of fine feathers. The White Plume Moth has a typical forewing that is divided into two lobes or "plumes," whilst its hindwing is divided into three. The lobes are covered with scales, just as those of other Lepidoptera are, and the addition of long fringe scales on each lobe adds to the feathery effect. The White Plume Moth holds its wings out when it rests, adopting a T shape; this is accentuated by its proportionally long, white hind legs, which trail alongside its abdomen.

CATERPILLAR: Olive-color body with yellow stripe along back and short spines. Feeds on bindweed

WINGSPAN: 1–1³⁄₈inches

HABITAT: Open grassland, hedgerows, roadsides, yards

RANGE: Across Europe into Asia

STATUS: Widespread and common

INDIAN MEAL MOTH

PLODIA INTERPUNCTELLA

The Indian Meal Moth is a member of the Pyralid family, known primarily as pest moths since their caterpillars will live amongst and consume stored grain products. The tiny nocturnal moth is attracted to light and can be seen flying inside houses. Its forewings are a copper color with pale gray toward the base. The hindwings are mottled gray and the body is a brownish gray. Its larvae eat a variety of stored products from cereals and grain to dried fruits, pet foods, and powdered milk. As it feeds its spins a silken thread which sticks food particles together in webs. It will also leave behind shed skin casts and its faeces, or frass. Caterpillars can often be seen hanging from ceilings on a single thread of silk.

CATERPILLAR: Pale body with black head
WINGSPAN: $^1/_2$–$^3/_4$ inch
HABITAT: Warehouses and most large food-storage facilities, kitchens
RANGE: Across North America, Europe and into Asia
STATUS: Very common

REGAL MOTH

CITHERONIA REGALIS

This attractive moth is known as both the Regal and the Royal Walnut Moth, and is a widespread representative of the Saturnid family in North America. Its forewings have a background color of gray-brown which is marked with ruddy orange veins, between some of which are pale yellow spots. The paler hindwing is more orange with smaller areas of gray toward the outer edge and a suffusion of yellow at the inner edge and base. Its large furred body is orange with pale yellow bands on the abdomen and yellow markings on the head and thorax. Its inability to feed means it only lives for a few days. Its slightly alarming caterpillar is commonly known as the Hickory Horned Devil.

CATERPILLAR: Green body with large branching head horns. Feeds on hickory and other broad leaves
WINGSPAN: 3½–6¼ inches
HABITAT: Woodland, forests, parks, and yards
RANGE: Across eastern states of the USA
STATUS: Generally common

PROMETHEA MOTH CALLOSAMIA PROMETHEAN

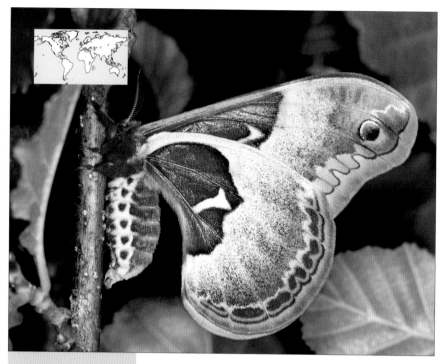

CATERPILLAR: Green body with four red horns on the back of the head and a red tail horn. Feeds on a variety of trees, including sassafras, poplar, and cherry

WINGSPAN: 3–4 inches

HABITAT: Deciduous forests, open woodland, orchards

RANGE: Eastern USA and south-east Canada

STATUS: Generally common

This American Saturnid or emperor moth comes in two distinctive sex forms. The males are a purplish-black color with a pale brown or tan border along both wings. The females are a red-brown color with pale wavy bands across both wings, a pale border marked with reddish lines on the forewing and a broken band on the hindwing. The female's body is red-brown and stocky, whereas the male's is slender and black. Both sexes bear a distinctive black eyespot with blue and white highlights in the tip of the forewing. Males fly during the afternoon and females at night—they meet to mate at dusk.

AUTOMERIS IO IO MOTH

Although the sexes of the Io Moth are colored differently, both bear startling eyespots on the hindwing which are effectively used to deter predators. When threatened, the Io Moth lifts its forewings to flash its "eyes." The smaller male is colored yellow on both wings, the pointed forewing has fine wavy lines of pale brown while the hindwing has a pair of parallel bands around the marginal edge. The large black and blue eyespot is in the center of the hindwing. The female has solid pale brown forewings and similar-colored hindwings, but with a broad white marginal band and a single black line around the eyespot.

CATERPILLAR: Pale green with stinging yellow spines in clusters along the back and red and white side stripes. Feeds on a variety of plants

WINGSPAN: 2–3³/₈ inches

HABITAT: Deciduous forests, open woodland, scrubland, fields, and yards

RANGE: From Canada into the USA toward Mexico

STATUS: Widespread and generally common

ATLAS MOTH

ATTACUS ATLAS

Although not as broad-winged as the Giant Agrippa Moth, the wings of the Atlas Moth have the biggest surface area, making this the world's largest moth. It is as distinctive as it is huge: the rich-brown wings are marked with fine white bands and translucent white triangular patches; the outer margins of both wings are paler brown with dark streaks and spots along the margin. The forewing tip is deeply curved and its patterning strongly resembles a snake's head with a small eyespot, a red slash for the mouth and pale shading. This deliberate feature deters predators very effectively. The caterpillar is almost as enormous as its moth, often reaching up to 4¾ inches in length.

CATERPILLAR: Green body with long spines covered with white sticky powder. Feeds on a variety of tree foliage, including willow and poplar
WINGSPAN: 6–12 inches
HABITAT: Tropical and subtropical woodland
RANGE: From India and Sri Lanka, across Indonesia to China
STATUS: Locally common, though numbers are declining

AMERICAN MOON MOTH

ACTIAS LUNA

This American member of the Actias sub-family is a beautiful and exotic moth, with its pale green wings and long, delicate tail streamers. It has relatively broad and stocky wings which are edged with red along both fore- and hindwings. The background color of the wings can vary between different regions, from a more yellow to a more blue green. The leading edge of the forewing is more broadly edged with dark, purplish gray. Both wings bear distinctive eyespots which earn it both its common and its scientific name. The sexes are similar, but the male's antennae are feathered. Mating pairs will often stay in position for up to twenty hours.

CATERPILLAR: Green body with raised pink spots. Feeds on tree foliage including alder, willow, and birch
WINGSPAN: 3–4³/₈ inches
HABITAT: Deciduous woodland
RANGE: Across North America, though fewer in Canada
STATUS: Generally common

INDIAN MOON MOTH ACTIAS SELENE

CATERPILLAR: Pale green body with red raised spots bearing black spines; two yellow spots on the head. Feeds on a variety of trees and shrubs, including rhododendron

WINGSPAN: $3^1/_8$–$4^3/_4$ inches

HABITAT: Tropical and subtropical woodland

RANGE: Across Asia into China

STATUS: Numerous in captivity, generally common in the wild

The Indian Moon Moth is a particular favorite of collectors and enthusiasts, and this has affected its numbers in the wild. Like all other Saturnid or emperor moths, this moth has no mouthparts and therefore lives for less than a week. It is however a striking moth and like the American Moon Moth has beautiful long tail streamers and pale yellow-green wings with distinctive eyespots. Its forewing is relatively narrow and slightly more pointed, edged with yellow on the outer margins and along the leading edge with reddish purple. The hindwing outer edge is more broadly yellow and this is continued down into the tail, which also bears a pinkish blush. The eyespots have a characteristic moon-like appearance.

SATURNIA PYRI GREAT PEACOCK MOTH

This big Saturnid moth is Europe's largest moth and is generally observed only in southern areas. It is mainly brown in coloring, with a rich brown background color on both wings. The forewing is dusted with white scales at the leading edge and the center; a dark band separates this from the solid brown base of the wing. A pale wavy band across the center of the forewing is repeated on the hindwing below the eyespot. The outer margins of both wings are bordered with white and buff. The hindwing is paler at the base and darker brown toward the outer edge. A black eyespot ringed with brown and black and highlighted white sits at the center of each wing.

CATERPILLAR: Pale green body with white side stripe, and raised hairy green spots. Feeds on fruit-tree foliage

WINGSPAN: 4–6 inches

HABITAT: Open woodland, orchards, and yards

RANGE: Southern Europe, into north Africa and Asia

STATUS: Common, considered a pest in orchards

POLYPHEMUS MOTH

ANTHERAEA POLYPHEMUS

In Greek mythology, Polyphemus was the giant with a single, all-seeing eye. The Polyphemus Moth is also particularly large with a very distinctive eyespot on the hindwing. The wing color varies from a pale yellow-brown to darker red-brown; the pattern is however regular. On both wings toward the base is a fine red line margined with white and toward the outer margins another fine brown line. The forewing bears a small white eyespot ringed with black and two dark patches at the tip. The hindwing has a large gray eyespot containing a yellow oval and ringed with black. The Polyphemus Moth is the most common member of the Saturnid family found in North America.

CATERPILLAR: Pale green body with raised red spots from which grow hairs. Feeds on tree foliage, particularly apple and hawthorn
WINGSPAN: 4–5 inches
HABITAT: A variety, including deciduous forests, desert canyons, scrubland and suburban yards
RANGE: Widespread across North America
STATUS: Generally common

EMPEROR MOTH
SATURNIA PAVONIA

CATERPILLAR: Pale green body with raised spots and yellow hairs. Feeds on heather, bramble and hawthorn
WINGSPAN: 2¼–3½ inches
HABITAT: Open woodland and clearings, meadows, and scrub
RANGE: Across Europe into Scandinavia
STATUS: Widespread and common

This daytime-flying, temperate moth can appear in different color forms in different areas; however all varieties share several key features. The background color of the Emperor Moth is either brown, light or dark, or a gray-brown, slightly mottled to enable camouflage. The outer margins of the forewing bear a broad white band, and the edge of the hindwing also has a pale border. A prominent eyespot is borne on each wing; the forewing eyespot sits on a contrasting patch of white whilst the hindwing eyespot sits on either a white or yellow patch depending on the variety. Like all Saturnid moths, the male has feathery antennae with which he can detect the scent of the female, often from a distance of over a mile.

CECROPIA/ROBIN MOTH
HYALOPHORA CECROPIA

Most Saturnid moths are able to produce silk, though not of the quality of the Bombycid moths, and in the USA the family is often referred to as Giant Silkmoths. The Cecropia is one of the biggest found in North America. It is an attractive brown and red moth; the background color of both wings is brown, with pale borders and a series of dark spots on the margin of the forewing which terminate at the tip with an eyespot. It has a crescent marking the center of each wing, and this is invariably white marked with red. A white and red band runs across both wings and the body is furred red, with a small white collar behind the head.

CATERPILLAR: Green with yellow back horns and blue markings. Feeds on tree and shrub foliage
WINGSPAN: 4¼–6 inches
HABITAT: Woodland, orchards, parks, and yards
RANGE: Widespread from Canada through USA
STATUS: Locally common, although declining as a result of pesticide use

HORNET MOTH

SESIA APIFORMIS

The Sesiidae family are best known for their mimicry of wasps, and the Hornet Moth is a particularly convincing example. Its large furred abdomen is striped with bands of yellow and black, and it has a yellow head and a black thorax edged with yellow sides. Its thickened antennae closely resemble those of a true hornet, as do its long, thick, brown hind legs. The Hornet Moth has transparent wings, typical for its family; the only wing scales are found on the brown edges. Although this is a daytime moth, it is rarely observed and its tree-boring caterpillar is widely considered a pest.

CATERPILLAR: Creamy white body. Feeds on the trunks and roots of poplar trees, taking up to two years to pupate
WINGSPAN: $1\frac{1}{8}$–$1\frac{3}{4}$ inches
HABITAT: Mature woodland, wooded marshland, and river valleys
RANGE: Across Europe into Asia, North America
STATUS: More common in warmer areas

DEATH'S HEAD HAWK MOTH
ACHERONTIA ATROPOS

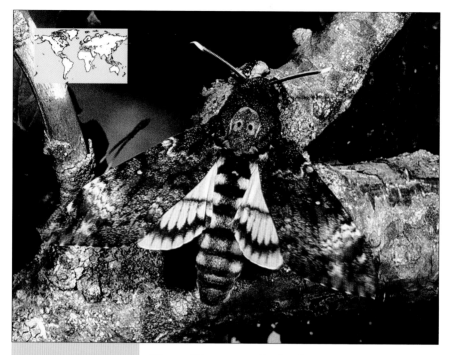

CATERPILLAR: Yellow body with blue-green bands and black side spots. Yellow tail spine. Feeds on potato leaves and deadly nightshade

WINGSPAN: 4–5 inches

HABITAT: Agricultural land, particularly potato fields; open grassland

RANGE: Across southern Europe into north Africa

STATUS: Generally common

This well known—indeed, infamous—moth earns its name from the unusual markings on its thorax, which resemble an image of a skull. It is the largest European example of a hawk or Sphingidae (sphinx) moth, a family of particularly large, powerful and fast fliers. Its forewings are dark brown mottled with light patches, and when at rest these cover the abdomen and the brighter, yellow hindwings. These are edged with a pair of brown bands, one broad and one fine, and this coloring is repeated on the abdomen, which is banded brown and yellow with a central back band in brown. Like its relative it has a long strong tongue, with which it can pierce beehives in search of honey. When threatened it will chirp.

HUMMINGBIRD CLEARWING
HEMARIS THYSBE

An attractive daytime moth, this American hummingbird moth closely resembles its European relative in all but its wings and its tail shape. Its body is a furred rusty brown color, with the lower part of the abdomen ringed with black and deep brown, terminating in a pointed, tufted tail. Its wings are clear, with dark, scaled tips and borders and black veining. The base of the wings is olive-green. The European *Macroglossum stellatarum* has solid-brown forewings, orange hindwings and a fanned tail. Both species so closely resemble hummingbirds when hovering in front of flowers that they are regularly mistaken for tiny birds.

CATERPILLAR: Green body with green and yellow tail horn. Feeds on hawthorn, viburnum, and honeysuckle

WINGSPAN: 1 $\frac{1}{2}$–2 $\frac{3}{8}$ inches

HABITAT: Open fields, meadows, hedgerows, roadsides

RANGE: Widespread from Alaska and Canada, through eastern USA to Colorado

STATUS: Very common

CAROLINA SPHINX

MANDUCA SEXTA

The wings of the Carolina Sphinx are mainly gray, mottled with black and white. This slightly dull appearance provides the moth with excellent camouflage against tree bark and rock. The hindwings have a more streaked pattern; however it is the abdomen that gives the moth is distinctive appearance, bearing six pairs of square yellow patches. The caterpillar of this moth is well known as a serious pest: it focuses particularly on plants such as tobacco, potato, and tomato and can attack crops in large numbers. It is for this reason that its pupa is commonly known as the tobacco hornworm.

CATERPILLAR: Green body with white side stripes and a red tail horn
WINGSPAN: 4–4¾ inches
HABITAT: Open farmland, scrubland, and yards
RANGE: Across the Americas, from northern states of the USA into South America
STATUS: Widespread and common

WEBBING/ COMMON CLOTHES MOTH

TINEOLA BISSELLIELLA

This tiny moth is capable of a great deal of destruction when left unchecked. Although the moth itself is not a pest, its larvae feed on all keratin-based materials such as wool, hair, and silk, as well as cotton, stored grain, and cereals. It therefore eats not only clothes, but carpets, and upholstery. As the larva feeds it weaves silken tubes and webs, inside which it lives, hence its other common name. The moth itself has pale, creamy wings and a similarly colored body. Its head is covered with red hair and it has proportionally long antennae. These moths are now rarely seen in houses, partly due to the drying effects of central heating and the extensive use of man-made fibers.

CATERPILLAR: Pale, whitish body with brown head
WINGSPAN: $^{3}/_{8}$–$^{3}/_{4}$ inch
HABITAT: In birds' nests and small animal dens. In cupboards, pipe lagging, or under carpets
RANGE: Across the northern hemisphere
STATUS: Widespread and common, though numbers in decline

MADAGASCAN SUNSET MOTH

CHRYSIRIDIA RIPHEARIA

This spectacular moth is a member of the Uraniid family; not only is it brightly colored with iridescent scaling and tail streamers, it is also a daytime flier and so is regularly mistaken for a butterfly. Found only on the island of its name, the Madagascan Sunset Moth has black forewings marked with luminous blue-green streaks and patches. The hindwings bear the "sunset," a red and orange patch which diffuses into a pale blue streak across the wing. The colors on the hindwing are marked with black patches and spots and the white streamers are lined with black. This moth has been highly sought after by collectors for hundreds of years, and during the nineteenth century its wings were often used to decorate jewelry.

CATERPILLAR: Yellow and black body with black hairs. Feeds on poisonous euphorbia plants
WINGSPAN: 3–4 inches
HABITAT: Tropical forests
RANGE: Confined to Madagascar
STATUS: Locally common